In
Visible
Ink

In
Visible
Ink

(crypto-frictions)

by

Aritha van Herk

NeWest Press
Edmonton

First edition

Canadian Cataloguing in Publication Data

Van Herk, Aritha, 1954-
  In visible ink

  (The Writer as Critic Series, 3)
  Includes bibliographical references and index.
  ISBN 0-920897-07-X

  1. Women and literature. I. Title. II. Series.
PN98.W64V35 1991   809'.89297   C91-091466-4

Credits
Design: Bob Young/BOOKENDS DESIGNWORKS
Editor for the Press: Smaro Kamboureli
Financial Assistance: NeWest Press gratefully acknowledges the
financial assistance of Alberta Culture and Multi-culturalism, The
Alberta Foundation for the Literary Arts, The Canada Council, and
The NeWest Institute for Western Canadian Studies.

Printed and Bound in Canada by
Hignell Printing Limited, Winnipeg

    NeWest Publishers Limited
    #310, 10359 - 82 Avenue
    Edmonton, Alberta
    T6E 1Z9

for Rudy Wiebe,
a reading lesson in reverse

Contents

∞ In Visible Ink *1*

∞ Blurring Genres: Fictioneer as Ficto-Critic *13*

∞ Extrapolations from *Miracles:* Out of Carol Shields *45*

∞ (no parrot/no crow/no parrot) *57*

∞ An Armchair (Reader's) Companion to Club Cars
and Ladies Crossing Canada by Train or Will the
Real Picara Please Leave Town (Please Haul Ass): Reading
Paulette Jiles' – Manual of Etiquette *69*

∞ Appropriations, The Salvation Army, and a Wager *85*

∞ Ghost Narratives: A Haunting *101*

∞ Nude Travelling: for Henry Kreisel *119*

∞ Of Viscera and Vital Questions *129*

∞ Stealing Inside After Dark *139*

∞ First the Chores and then the Dishes *157*

∞ Writing the Immigrant Self: Disguise and Damnation *173*

∞ A Re/quisition on Death: Reading *Cassandra 191*

Works Cited *211*

Index *217*

Acknowledgements

Some of these pieces have been previously published, and grateful acknowledgement is hereby made to the journals where they first appeared. Some have been read at conferences. I confess to much dissatisfied revision and re-inscription.

"An Armchair (Reader's) Companion to Club Cars and Ladies Crossing Canada by Train or Will the Real Picara Please Leave Town (Please Haul Ass)" first appeared in *The Malahat Review*, 83 (Summer 1988): 115-126.

"Blurring Genres: Fictioneer as Ficto-Critic" was first given as separate papers at two conferences, The Blurring Genres Conference in Calgary, Alberta (April 1989), and Toward a History of the Literary Institution V in Edmonton, Alberta (November 1988).

"Extrapolations from *Miracles*" first appeared in *Room of One's Own*, 13, 1 & 2 (July 1989): 99-108.

"First the Chores and then the Dishes" first appeared in *Psychological Perspectives*, 23 (1990): 38-48.

"Ghost Narratives: a Haunting" first appeared in *Open Letter*, 7, 9 (Winter, 1991): 61-70.

"(no parrot/no crow/no parrot)" first appeared in *Prairie Fire*, 8, 4 (Winter 1987-88): 12-20.

"Of Viscera and Vital Questions" first appeared in *Language in Her Eye: Writing and Gender*. Toronto: Coach House Press, 1990: 272-278.

"Stealing Inside After Dark" first appeared in *The Journal of Educational Thought/Revue de la Pensée Educative*, 24, 3A (December 1990): 34-45.

"Writing the Immigrant Self: Disguise and Damnation" first appeared in *The Dutch in North-America: their immigration and cultural continuity.* Amsterdam: VU University Press, 1991: 154-164.

There are many people to whom I would like to express gratitude:

Smaro Kamboureli, for her sagacious editing, and the generous discernment that has made the writing in this book much better.

Nicole Markotic, for her careful research and reading.

The Calgary Institute for the Humanities, whose Research Fellowship enabled me to write steadily and without interruption. I especially want to thank Gerry Dyer and Cindy Atkinson for their excellent support.

Robert Sharp, for his unflagging belief in me.

Terry and Bezal Jesudason of Resolute Bay, for their northern expediting.

Abraham Pijamini of Grise Fiord, simply for being Pijamini.

In
Visible
Ink

It is May. In the ordinary world, beyond these ridges of ice, beyond the edge of the Arctic Ocean, below the tree line, below the imaginary dashes of the Arctic Circle, it is spring: all the snow gone, the cold vanished in wait for next year's winter, and the sun a long light retiring into evening. This is the time of blackthorn winter, a metaphorical cold of the second week in May, unreal as this freezing surround is not.

It is the second week of May and I am sitting on the back of a komatik riding over the frozen Arctic Ocean. Everywhere that my eye reaches is dazzling snow, implacable ice, a white/blue/white/blue configuration of polar sea. The blue is not water but old, old ice, ice that has floed and shifted, that continually grinds against itself, that has never thawed, that will not melt for years. To the far edges of my seeing is frozen ocean, no skating smooth expanse but choppy with ridges, broken, a nordic goddess's tumbled cake pans.

I am travelling over this broken water, chopped and corrugated and firm as ground. The komatik I ride is not a comfortable mode of transportation. The traditional Inuit sledge, pulled by a snarlingly avid snowmobile, it bounces and bangs, rises precariously over icy ledges to slam down on the snow beyond. I am jarred to the very bone, the komatik creaking and groaning

1

through this rutted and unpolished ice whose ironbound surface breaks and breaks.

And yet, in this distant, eerie world of ice, unwriting and unwritten, merely a cipher of human bone and blood, I am inexplicably, immeasurably happy: because I am finally free of words.

The Inuit make little distinction between land and water. In the extreme Arctic, living with an ocean that cracks open into water for only a few short months a year, they move from land to ice and ice to land with assurance of both's accessibility, opportunity for food and water and even shelter. For the Inuit, *the land* does not end where ocean begins: it only begins there. The ocean and its creatures are still the primary source of their survival. It is to the sea, its bountifulness, that the people of the north go. Inland is no preferred concept. There is ice and there is land. They are both, despite their fundamental difference, covered with snow. They are both consummate empagements, intagli in the white of this endless folio.

May is relatively warm – between twenty and ten below – and the Arctic sun keeps itself up for twenty-four hours, although it drops low on the horizon between ten at night and two in the morning. May is a good month for hunting seal, which come onto the ice to bask beside their holes. It is a good month to travel, before the ice breaks up. And I am travelling, by snowmobile and komatik, from Resolute Bay on Cornwallis Island to Grise Fiord (the most northerly of Canadian communities), on Ellesmere Island. Only Eureka and Alert lie farther north than Grise Fiord, and they are white man's stations (not settlements because no one lives there permanently), one a weather station and the other an army base.

You, reader, are entitled to wonder why I am doing this.

This journey's conditions are no more luxurious than riding in a komatik is comfortable. In order to stay warm, I wear five layers of clothing, I huddle beneath a caribou skin, and at night, I sleep on that same caribou skin. The clothing I wear is of Inuit design, my kamiks warmer than any southern boot could imagine itself. Still, it is significantly below zero and wind intensifies the cold. Out on the open ice, the Arctic temperature prods every nerve, every bone. A reminder of where I am, and that who I am does not matter a writ in this cryptically enduring world.

I am not motivated by destination, although I appear to be enacting a journey: travelling between Resolute Bay and Grise Fiord. But departure and arrival are of no consequence. The six hundred odd kilometres we meander, the five days and nights we spend moving around Dungeness Point on Cornwallis Island, up Wellington Channel, across Devon Island, down Viks Fiord to Bear Bay, then across Jones Sound to South Cape on Ellesmere Island may offer the illusion of travel, but are essentially the measurements of measurement-obsessed man in the south. I know that when I return to my home in Calgary I will be bombarded with questions of measurement: how long did the trip take? how far did you go? how cold was it? Such determinations are meaningless here; they are completely effaced by the articulation of each moment's essense, this hereness, this nowness, and nothing else. I am suspended in an Arctic, not near Arctic or high Arctic but extreme Arctic, beyond all writing and its romance, beyond the intellectual comprehension or the geographical experience of most of those people calling themselves Canadians. I am simply here, reduced to *being*, breathing the ice-crystal air through my nose and into my lungs, stamping my feet against the granular snow to revive my circulation. I am at last beyond language, at last literately invisible.

Which is, reader, I confess, the state I ideally wish to attain. Finally, finally, in a life dominated by language, I am to some degree free of it, of having to speak and read and write. If you have read *Places Far From Ellesmere*, you know that the time I spent at

Lake Hazen in the northern part of Ellesmere Island taught me unreading, the act of dismantling a text past all its previous readings and writings. The landscape there, its delicious remoteness, calm unmeasurability, catalyzed my reading act into something beyond reading, enabling me to untie all the neatly laced up expectations of words and their printing, their arrangement on the page, the pages bound together into a directive narrative, that then refused to be static, but turned and began to read back, to read me, to unread my very reading and my personal geography. But reader, that was summer, however brief.

And yes, I always want to go farther, push back another boundary, cross another invisible line. Yes, reader, what I am about to confess is heresy, but I long, finally, to escape the page, to escape ink and my own implacable literacy, altogether.

Yes, I am anxious about reading, that I will always have something (enough) to read, that I will always have satisfying words for company, that I will never be stranded without a book, an addiction to reading the intimacies of language caressed by others. I am anxious about writing, that I will always find words to articulate my intellectual transgressions, the ideas I circle and circle, watching and writing. I force the two together, write about my reading, read my writing, refuse to function without one or the other implicated in some way, even if only silently, secretly, in my head. The conspiracies of bibliophilism. I book my world, I word all possible collisions and encounters, I am enslaved to language, and I enslave my experience to language. Visible ink.

But reader, I am not complaining, not in distress. I do not dismiss language as primary and pivotal function, nor do I subscribe to the naive temptations of anti-intellectualism. Literacy is a powerful talisman; I do not decry its magic, and I hold it the most precious skill of my life. My reading and writing sustain me beyond sustenance: they are both life and livelihood. Thus important enough for me to recognize that I should deprive –

hardly even possible! – myself of them, even for a short time, to understand more completely their consequence in my life.

So reader, I have freed myself from words – at least, written and read words. For the first time since I learned to read at the age of five (and I am thirty-seven now) I am spending five days without reading a word, holding my breath. Although I took books with me to Resolute Bay, muttered and mumbled and weighed them in my hand and turned them upside-down, I am now on the frozen reaches of the Arctic Ocean with no signs to signify for me, invisibled to print. And while the pedant will argue that there is always oral and mental language, that we carry our signs and their signifiers with us, that I am reading this Arctic I am suspended in; while you may be right that I struggle to find some corresponding signs to articulate my experience, ultimately this page of Arctic is not written or read by insignificant me. No, it (agent) reads and writes me. I am its text, impressionable, inscribable, desirous of contamination, a page open to its tattoo, marking.

How to describe or even begin to evoke this landscape? Reader, it occupies the realm of magic, a terrifying ecstasy. This world *is* beauty without adornment, beyond imagined possibility into almost hallucinatory beguilement. Here is a strange combination of mirage-like airiness and abiding perpetuity, a lapidification of fluidity both physically daunting and terrifyingly lovely. So thin, so meager language seems in its capacity to re-cite this sublimity. Overwhelmed by this daunting and indifferent and resplendent Arctic, my paltry language is finally insufficient. I am merely filled with a wonder beyond wonder, invisibled by awe.

When we bump off Cornwallis Island and onto the ice, Resolute Bay quickly fades to a visual handful of coloured dust. No boundary crossed, a seemingly limitless surface tempting entrance, we are reduced to infinitesimal punctuation marks. The wind against my stinging face adjuratory breath, cold suffusing time.

Young seal sunning on the ice are still furry and gaze pure

curiosity. Their open holes blue circles indiscernible in the blue snow around them, camouflaged as their black bodies are not. They slip into those apertures as slickly as their bodies' shape, phocine. The rough zigzagging of our path, ice blocks like chunks of cake thrust into blue and green pressure ridges. The komatik slams itself over a crease, then rises again and on a quick turn drives itself up against a huge block of ice, the runners stuck fast on either side. The snowmobile crescendoes fruitlessly, we climb out and back the komatik off, then push, heave it over the ridge. Right wooden runner cracked by the impact. Keep going, and at the next smooth spot we stop, Pijamini neatly saws a plywood piece to fit, nails from a tin, hammers the runner back to strength. Rough ice. Push more than we ride, climbing in and out of the komatik an ordeal wearing so many clothes, the cold cold, the sun hot. Bannock dipped in hot tea. And again buckled ice, huge scrawling chunks that we inconceivably thread, intricate reading of passage a reminder that we are not travelling but static, finally arrested here, in the ice-landscape. And polar bear tracks, crossing before our tracks, lines of intersection conspicuous for their rarity (Wiebe, *Playing Dead* 50), but here not rare, a veritable highway for the golden-white sovereign (*Thalarctus maritimus*) patrolling the broken ridges for absent-minded or sleeping seal. Stunningly huge, full-muscled and furred, moving effortlessly through the rough ice. Slows, walks, looks at us, scoops snow with his mouth, ambles away. Tracks, tracks, one bear days ago, a mother and two cubs a few hours ago, tracks, tracks, the creases of their padded feet clear as character, imprinted on the snow. Markings: claw marks on the ice side of an iceberg. And tracks, tracks, polar bear tracks followed by fox tracks, following the possibility of dozing seal, their flipper marks around ocean breathing holes. Our komatik tracks following themselves into tracklessness and invisibility. Writings of passage. Pressure ridges, lines where the ocean meets itself and forces its own force upwards. The tide under the ice, currents below solidity. Colophons.

I sleep on this cryptic and indifferent ocean. No hull between us, only solid solid ice, and the thin sail of a double-walled tent. Below me a down sleeping bag, then caribou skin, then foamy, then tent floor, then four inches of snow, then six feet of ice, then five hundred feet of freezing polar water cold as a fist; yet rich with fish, seal, whales, shrimp. They bump their noses against my sleeping skin, this sleep without dreams, without sign or reference, measureless and deep. Here or now invisible and unfathomable. Only sleeping. Written into sleep.

The komatik creaks and groans like an old ship battling high seas. Made of wood now (once bone and moss, skin and sinew and ice), but still lashed together only with rope, no nails. Pliable and resilient, it seems almost supple in its tracking of the snowmobile, giving into the jarring tilts and plunges of the fractured ice. And land no smoother in its dips and curves, banks under the runners, Devon Island wet and heavy with snow, even the cliffs jagged, and the sharp hooves of the elegant caribou, fleet as a sentence, a distant conjunction. Muskoxen lower their heads at us over a hill, then turn and drag their tracks away. Moss under the snow, and rock, screelings of gravel, emerging to stark cliffs as encarved as Egypt's Abu Simbel and then ice again, a different phonation, ringing faintly under our runners.

There is hoarfrost on the snow, crystals of snow growing on snow, dazzling yellow and blue under the sun. Intricate, delicate rime of a cryological aesthetic, blades sometimes an inch long, and every frostflake exquisite construction. And patches of ice-fog, the contours of land and ice surreal disappearance, the komatik floating silently through silence, and I see grain elevators, caragana hedges, the parkland around the Battle River miraged onto this arctic. Reader, I have almost left myself behind, and in this ice-fog read my own erasure, written and engraved past, the language I am slave to made invisible. We drift eerily, and I cannot be sure if I sleep or wake, if we are suspended or moving. Still, when I lean over the komatik's side, the air rushes against my face, and I hear the steady hiss of the runners along the snow, another passing. Sundogs refract on either side of the glaring sun that my dark glasses cannot diminish. An omen surely, a reading of the snow and its polar perhelion, constituent activity. Warning or blessing, guide or direction? No sign. A polar body, coordinate, codeclination? Where am I? Vanished, effaced, unwritten. Invisibled.

Yes, reader, I have cited space and measurement, time and quotidian gesture, all in vain. I cannot read these reaches. I have no language for *arctic*, impossible to convey to you the sensation of stepping from a sleeping bag warm with night breath into an eagerly frigid weatherglass. I cannot measure polar bear tracks, or describe to you the habits of sunning seals. I am quite simply unable to write of or through this polar spell. Instead, it inscribes me, takes over my cullible imagination and its capacity for words: invents me for its own absent-minded pleasure. Effaces my referentiality, a transformation without continuity or chronology. I am re-invented by a great white page. Not *isolation* but complete invisibility, all causes and destinations blurred by causes other to causalities I believe I know.

And now know I do not know.

Even more extreme is the illusion of absence that is truly presence, tremendous presence, with no need to articulate itself narcissistically, being so much a *hereness*. This space, this landscape, this temperature, question all *document* and instead document me, without reference to an other; decipherable as glass I am, and fragile as any silenced voice, a tracement of arctic essence. No comparisons possible, no contrast available for measurement or ruler for diversity. This north is the gauge, and all else divergence. I am effaced, become an enunciative field, a page untouched by pen, no archive and no history. Happily.

Ah reader, what discourse is this? A snowmobile's diminished whine? The snowhiss of runners, the creak and groan of a labouring komatik, bouncing over what is not a smooth page of snow but a rough-toothed, jagged dimension, continually broken and interrupted by itself? As I am now, profoundly interrupted, disinherited of all that locates my literate self. Lost to text and language, become finally merely a text to be written. A flimsy alphabet. I could believe I have found the north in my own head (Wiebe, *Playing Dead* 113).

No, it has found me.

I wake in the morning to Pijamini's voice talking on the radio in the cooktent. He talks to Annie, whose husband he is, in Grise Fiord. The soft, throaty Inuktitut syllables bridge sleep and wakefulness, and signify morning – or is it afternoon, or evening? Time not measurable either, we seem to be getting up around two in the afternoon and travelling all night, but watches mean and matter nothing. Pijamini's voice speaks me into existence, creates my ears again. Huskily sibilant, his language in its rhythmic rise and fall delineates both where and who I am, unwritten here on the thick blue ice of the Arctic Ocean. Pijamini is short and solid, almost tiny, but his strength is powerfully obvious, despite his age, sixty-four, he says with a grin. He is the leader, the most experienced person on this becalmed journey, and I ride in the komatik pulled by his snowmobile. How well he reads this invisible world, his body itself a signage, *polar* and *north* contained in his posture. He climbs icebergs to survey his north, then unerringly proceeds through the most impenetrable of ice fields.

He understands and speaks very simple (what does that mean, uncomplicated, uncluttered?) English, but he is at first shy, silent. Only after hours of pushing the komatik over rough ice, after I sight the first polar bear, does he say a word to me. I am ashamed that I use this rough, barbaric language, ashamed that I can speak to him only in the coldness of English, that I know no Inuktitut. I do not want to speak English with him, I want to talk to him in *his* language, the language of this overwhelming snowworld. I say nothing, smile only, push the komatik when it gets stuck. And then, in a sudden moment of desire, I ask him the Inuit word for sun. He tells me, poker-faced, a little curiously, and when I repeat it, he laughs. My epiglottal Dutch for once gives me some pronunciative advantage. "You speak good Inuktitut," he says. "Very good."

Reader, even invisibled to language, one makes what signs one can. I place my dwarfed foot in the foot-writing left by a polar bear. I circle every iceberg three times, on my right, reading myself a spell. And Pijamini names his world for me: cloud, sun, falling snow, snow on the ground, ice, bear, tracks, caribou, muskox, sundogs, iceberg, seal. He names his family to me, his seven children and their children. He names the points, the promontories, the edges of the islands as we pass. I repeat his namings, carefully shaping my mouth and tongue around their inflections and contours, and Pijamini laughs. "Very good, very good. You should come to Grise Fiord, study Inuktitut." He gives me *his* words, and thus names me, writes my invisible and unlanguaged self into his archaeology. I am written, finally, with that nomadic language.

Reader, reading you, I know you want me to put those words down here, reveal their magic incantation. Never. They are Pijamini's words, not mine, and if I was able to hear them and to mimic them, it was only through his agency. I will not raid them, or repeat them beyond the Arctic sea, beyond the secret worlds of ice. They gave me a reading, read me in that space where I, trying to read anew, was finally written. Reader, this amulet of the first and most final of all crypto-frictions is that one can be disappeared and re-written in a language beyond one's own. Herein resides the ultimate illusion of text: you are not reading me but writing, not me but yourself; you are not reading writing but being read, a live text in a languaging world.

And yes, reader, in this cold May where I am finally freed from words, I am given a different text to carry south with me, to this oh so visible place full of words shouting everywhere, demanding to be read. In the silence after text dies, I will hear, somewhere in my buried polar ear, the soft Inuit voice of Pijamini naming the world in Inuktitut, and laughing.

Blurring Genres:

Fictioneer as Ficto-Critic

I. Beginning: Fictioneer versus Buchaneer

Georg Lukacs maintains that the novel is "the epic of an age in which the extensive totality of life is no longer directly given, in which the immanence of meaning in life has become a problem, yet which still thinks in terms of totality" (56). If he is right, and pretend for a moment that he is, then the critic of that genre, or fiction itself, has the deliciously self-righteous task of preacher/reader to an amoral congregation of fictioneers, engaged in "the most hazardous genre" (73). Paul Hernadi's gentle adaptation is a nudge toward construction: "literary genres are, or at least can be, helpful guides to writers as conventional frames" (21). Or Pierre Kohler's monetaristic currency: "the genres are the economy of the arts and letters" (137-9), a process of ordering that begins with selection and results in construction. Stephen Dedalus a.k.a. James Joyce has genre almost literally stacked: "you will see that art necessarily divides itself into three forms progressing from one to the next. These forms are: the lyrical form, the form wherein the artist presents his image in immediate relation to himself; the epical form, the form wherein he presents his image in mediate relation to himself and to others; the dramatic form, the form wherein he presents his image in immediate relation to others" (213-14). And Joyce is backed up by critics too numerous for enlistment. Until Tzvetan Todorov, who sees individual genres as mere ciphers to the larger genre of literature (13).

The fictioneer lives within a category, a biological species, a generic assignation. Prose, poetry, drama: a world in triplicate. A condition of being that the book must genre itself, must delineate its boundaries. But the rigid stratifications of canonical thought invite transgression, especially here, beyond the border of anywhere, in this generic of the post-partum, post-modern, post-colonial, post-patriarchal, post-mortem, and thus pre – . But that is a tantalizing unknown.

Sinfulness invites damnation but lawlessness is its own temptation, and in this age of high-tech theory, the fictioneer has scant defense but to become an outlaw of words, on the lam and on the run. Out of self-defense, she can only invent crypto-friction as ficto-critic.

One Hannike Buch, the ficto-critic under examination, has done her homework. Hannike Buch is an outlaw, has outlawed herself in her appropriations, in her refusals and her rebounds. She is every fictioneer's nightmare. She takes over in the game of buchaneer versus fictioneer. No contest. Buch always wins.

She writes this stuff, whatever it might be called, this ficto-crypticism, under an assumed name, a name that has its own peculiar history, that she unearthed or took on seven, maybe eight years – whatever historiographical time period – ago, when she began to write ficto-criticism, careful about spoiling her fictional reputation – no, get that straight, not her fictional reputation, her fiction's reputation. Her fiction didn't want her committing infidelities (genre crime) with other forms. The fictioneer was in Stavanger, Norway, at an Arts Festival, giving a reading, giving a talk, making fiction, sneaking out at night to listen to the festival's best component, imported American jazz, black and smoky, having to sneak out under the disapproving eyes of the hotel porter, and no one in the world can look so disapproving as a Norwegian hotel porter, they've practised, the fictioneer has first-hand knowledge. A chubby little Norwegian writer was following her around, scared shitless but determined, you have to give him that. He wanted to sleep with a Canadian writer. Believe it or not, she scares most of them, except that being afraid only made him more determined. Nor did he deter her, she wanted to listen to jazz, but instead she was seated next to another visiting writer (see how that moment slid past, no generic responsibility for *deus ex machina* at all), who was on the programme but whom she hadn't yet met, and whose books, she was embarrassed to say, she had not read. Although he was not old, he walked with a cane and a limp, his hair was peppering itself into middle age (good thing this isn't a creative writing class or you would complain that characterization depends on more than grey hair and an ambiguous limp), and he was in the despicable habit of smoking smelly cigars. All of which she was willing to forgive for his eyes – yes, that old cliché, his eyes, which had the extraordinary intensity of periwinkle knives. The only eyes like it, that she had ever seen, were the eyes of the boy-actor who played Oskar in *The Tin Drum* (but that might be another cliché) – all of which she was willing to forgive for his eyes and his name.

The saxophone was grieving with that rough-sided, tongue-licking asphalt layer it gets in the thick of the night, so she didn't think she had heard correctly when they were introduced, she looked at him and at his eyes and she simply disbelieved. Which is, and this is the moment for a stage whisper, when most people would know they were in trouble, when she should have known she *will be* in fictional trouble.

The next day (a nice elision here containing the rest of the night before, including its persistant Norwegian writer), they were introduced again, and this time, no saxophone, no smoke, no grumble of other voices, no importunate Norwegian writer, she *had* to hear his name. He stuck out his hand and repeated himself.

"Buch," he said. "Pleased to meet you, again. We met last night at the jazz concert."

She stared at him. "What?" (The old Canadian vernacular, it sneaks into as many genres as it can.)

"Buch," he said softly, "Hans-Christof Buch."

Now, the fictioneer is not a jealous woman, she has never felt jealous of anyone, but at that moment, she positively rippled with a great spasm of envy, or covetousness, and she lost her tongue, couldn't think of a word to say except to mutter a kind of syllabic incredulity. Between knives in the eyes and a name like that, she was struck dumb. But there were five or six people standing around, they always are, watching, checking out potential genre violations, so she had to come up with something, and she actually stammered the truth.

"I envy your name," she said. "Is it really your name? Your real name?" Note first that she did not say, "I envy you your name," which might have been more grammatically correct, but technically wasn't, she spoke the truth; and second, her doubting of the reality of Buch, his name at least. Surely he would have had to invent himself a name like that, take it on, assume it, some element of artificiality involved. She was beside herself with jealousy; imagine, she thought, *being born a Buch.*

He laughed. "Yes," he said, "*Buch* is my name."

"Oohh," she said regretfully, just like that, green-eyed longing obvious as hell. "I wish I had your name."

And one of the five or six interested observors, the genre police, the ones watching, following, taking notes, trying to sneak a hand into a pocket, giving advice, moral or otherwise, free, unasked for, but who practise their own doubled standards, said, "You could marry him."

"Certainly," said Buch gently. "Then it is yours." He knew all about subverting the police, through readily contravenable rules.

Now, the fictioneer had never read Hans-Christof Buch in her life (although she was very well-read): she only envied him his name. But the spontaneous wedding, which became something of a celebrated event at that famous arts festival in Stavanger, Norway, was more or less enacted according to genre regulations. There was a great search for an official who could perform the name ceremony in English, the one language both shared, since the fictioneer did not speak German and Buch did not speak Dutch, and neither spoke nor understood Norwegian. Finally, the suddenly helpful Norwegian writer (who had been determined to sleep with a Canadian) came up with someone (a woman pretending to be the mayor of Stavanger but actually an opera singer in disguise), and the writer received official sanction to call herself Hannike Buch.

This appropriation could be considered a cheat, but usage is the real test of a name, and Hannike Buch cryptos ficto-criticism left and right, the fictioneer can't shut her up or down, and she is the real author of this text, as well as the book of ficto-criticism (*A Frozen Tongue*) that the fictioneer is supposed to have published by now.

You, reader, would like to go backwards and unearth the end of the marriage tale, a hint of whether or not that peculiar conjunction was ever consummated, but that is another story, in a different genre. Suffice to say that Hans-Christof Buch, he of the enviable name, is a fine German novelist, that *The Wedding at Port-au-Prince*, his best known novel, was written long before their presumably bigamous exchange, since both the fictioneer and he were already married (something the Norwegians were quite willing to overlook), and has nothing whatsoever to do with Stavanger. But Hannike Buch becomes more and more a refugee, an intrusion, an alibi. She has a toughness and resilience that Aritha van Herk lacks; she is her own genre, and her assumption of the guise of critic rather than fictioneer tells you something about her priorities. She knows what she is doing, far better than van Herk does. It might also interest you, reader, to know that there are exactly two *Buchs* in the Calgary telephone directory. In that same directory or phone book, there are also two *Books*, but theirs is not a name the fictioneer aspires to. The fictioneer is swayed by the idea of forbearance, and Gutenberg's German seems a necessary and additional signification to signage.

So Hannike Buch does van Herk's homework, she looks everything up. She finds the fictioneer a trilingual *Bibliography of the Poetics of Literary Genres* by one Wolfgang Ruttkowski. That bibliographer isn't kidding; he's done his homework too, spent years dis/ and re/covering genre. Trilingual triplication carried to its ultimate degree, he even apologizes for missing a few, and he's found one hundred and forty groupings, genre gone wild, proliferating in subgenres, as though the sub, itself a species, will keep them safe; and what can any genre undertake except endless propagation? Todorov too assists: "Where do genres come from? Quite simply from other genres" (15). Buch is determined that texts be divided into genres until there is no genre anymore, perhaps no words even, all cut too fine, and nothing left but a great blur. Blurring genres.

Buch is the fictioneer's alter ego, her double, her doppelgänger. Now there's a salacious genre, that of the double, the mirror image, Narcissus. To any bookish life that purports singularity in direction if not practice, the crypto-critic comes. She is intent, as doubles always are, on crime, not only confronting but usurping the genred position of the fictioneer. Rumour has it that a meeting with the double presages death. The double re/places the writer. You do not need to bed down with a treatise on Joseph Conrad's "The Secret Sharer" for the ficto-critic to move in on the fictioneer in this ficto-piece – not story, not criticism, not buch, not generic enough to be counted as one thing or another.

Hannike Buch is your buchaneer of ficto-criticism, the double of your fictioneer, Aritha van Herk, who subscribes, most emphatically, or so she claims, to fiction. The fictioneer is willing to recognize the existence of genre, its usefulness, its rules to write by. The fictioneer wishes that Buch would get lost, move out, the cabin's too small for two. Every time she comes in the door, Buch ambushes her with an eraser, with a new pair of glasses. All the lines are blurring.

Buch wields Ruttkowski's weaponed recitation, relentless in its manifold dis/genre:

> *Literary Dictionaries/ Genres in General/*
> *Akrostichon/ Allegorie/ Almanach / Anagramm/*
> *Anekdote/ Anstandsbuch/Aphorismus/ Atellane/*
> *Bänkelsang/ Ballade/ Entwicklungsroman/*
> *Biographie/ Bispel/ Brief(gedicht)/ Briefroman/*
> *Burleske/ Chanson/ Chor/ Comics/ Commedia*
> *dell'arte/ Detektivroman,Kriminalliteratur/ Dialog/*
> *Didaktik/ Drama/ Drehbuch/ Duodrama/ Einakter/*
> *Ekloge/ Elegie/ Emblemliteratur/ Epigramm/ Epilog/*
> *Episches Theater/ Epos,Epik/ Epyllion/*
> *Erbauungsliteratur/ Erzählung/ Essay, Artikel/*
> *Exempel/* (15)

When the fictioneer comes home from a conference on genre, Buch is waiting inside the door, ready to slam the fictioneer with a list of genres, all intended to prove that there is no such thing, that genre has subverted itself. Buch is fire-eyed, accusatory. "You're doing it again," she cries, "fooling around with the temptations of genre. You think it will give you an answer. You think it will write your next book, all that stuff about helpful guides to writers, about having the tension of form to inspire you."

"But fiction is my *métier*," says the fictioneer, with real bewilderment and not a little exhaustion.

"Tough," says Buch, and goes through the fictioneer's collection of books, crossing out van Herk and writing *Buch* on the flyleaf, every one of them transgressed by the de-genred book, its volumized braggadocio. "Let this be a lesson to you," she says to the fictioneer. "*Buch, Buch, Buch.* Just *buch*, nothing else."

The fictioneer shrugs. "I don't care what you write in my books. It's only defacement. You still can't change my story."

Buch quotes Robert Kroetsch, as elicited by Shirley Neuman and Robert Wilson. "Criticism is really a version of story, you see; I think we are telling the story to each other of how we get at story. It is the story of our search for story" (30). She continues, "My job is to *buch* you, to make you cross lines and cross them out. Reading is an act of ficto-criticism, even if the book you are reading is Buch's book. You have to learn to refuse the comfort of category. Where have you left your noodles?"

"You sound like my mother," says the fictioneer.

"I am better," says Buch. "I am your buchaneer."

The fictioneer has to sneak out to her office to practise genre, and even then she catches herself looking over her shoulder. Buch is ubiquitous, she has a penetrating voice that lays its nose down on the page and sniffs contemptuously. Buch infiltrates the fictioneer's text, its narrative and characters and atmosphere, its dialogue and action. Buch's gang hangs around the margins all the time, pretending to be first one genre and then another, as if to stress how easy form is. And they inhabit theft, the buchaneers, stealing a few lines here, a few characteristics there, blend them all together, and say, "See, there are no boundaries discernible here."

And Buch's recitation of Ruttowski continues:

Fabel/ Farce, Facetie/ Fastnachtspiel/ Fernsehspiel/ Festspiel/Feuilleton/ Film/ Flugblatt/ Formel/ Fragment –

(Buch interrupts herself, she likes this one, maintains that it has spirit, a clean record, and what is it doing in this bad company?)

> – *Frauenlied/ Gassenhauer/ Gelegenheitsdichtung/*
> *Geschichte einer Jugend/ Geschichtsschreibung/*
> *Ghasel/ Groteske/ Happening/ Hausväterliteratur/*
> *Heimatkunst/ Heldendictung/ Heroide/*
> *Herolddichtung/ Himmelsbrief/ Hörspiel/*
> *Humoreske/ Idylle/ Kalender/ Kantate/ Kanzone/*
> *Kasside/ Kasus/ Kinderlied/ Kirchenlied/ Komödie/*
> *Kreuzzugsliteratur/ Kritik, Rezension/*
> *Kurzgeschichte/ Laienspiel/ Legende/ Leich/ Libretto/*
> *Lied, Arie/ Litanei/ Liturgie/ Lobgedicht/ Lügendichtung/*
> *Lyrik/ Maccaronische Dichtung/ Madrigal/*
> *Madonnendichtung/ Märchen/ Maere/ Maskerade/*
> *Meistersang/ Melodrama/ Memorabile/ Mimus/ Minnesang/*
> *Monodrama/ Monolog/ Musical/ –* (15-16)

"Stop," says the fictioneer, holding her head. "Enough already. Benedetto Croce here we come. He was a fanatic, Buch, he was just reacting. They all over-turned him." [Croce's 1922 *Aesthetic* objects to all generic distinctions, on the basis that "He who begins to think scientifically has already ceased to contemplate aesthetically" (36), and that every true work breaks generic laws. He resolutely forwards the uniqueness of every work of art, hence his objection to the violence of categorization. Hernadi claims Croce is reacting to the excessive positivism and historicism of the generation preceding (12), but in a post-Derridean and post-Barthian literary world we can no longer scoff at Croce's distrust. He is their father, a forerunner of Heather Dubrow's argument that "since the reader is faced with an infinite series of conflicting signals and codes, it is almost impossible to interpret a work of literature precisely and objectively. Hence, . . . the codes that in theory might help us to read the text – including genre – are in practice virtually irrelevant." (85)] So much for the distinctions of the square-bracket digression.

"And now we're overturning him," says Buch. "Isn't it a good thing we can re-read books? At least we can rectify our mistakes by re-figuring the story."

"You are impossible," says the fictioneer. "You want to rob me of what order and shape there is to my art, if not my life."

"Art! Life! You need to learn how to evade plot, my dear," says Buch. "I am the alter to your ego, and I am standing here, vibrating like a cello behind a great bunch of funereally-arranged flowers, trying to convince you that genre is something like a long line of nicely varnished but implacable coffins ready to slam their lids down on you, alive or dead, the moment you choose one."

"Charlie Chaplin, here we come." (The fictioneer is getting tired of this sustained abuse. She is trying to finish a novel.)

But Buch refuses to sympathize. "Do you know how many genres there are out there? Any one of them could finish you off."

"You've been listing them for me. Your categories tromp through my writing all the time."

But Buch will not take the blame, insists that there is no genre in tromping or stomping either, for that matter. "Listen," she says, "let me tell you about stamps and government glue, and where they position you."

"No," says the fictioneer, "don't start on the Canadian postal system."

"Just hold on and listen," says Buch. "Okay, there's this woman who goes to her doctor for a check-up, a routine pelvic, right."

"Oh no," says the fictioneer, "not a medical story."

"Shut up. This is important. And it's not like *Dead Ringers* either. She goes to her doctor for her yearly pap smear, it's all very much above board, she likes her doctor, her doctor likes her, maybe because her doctor is a woman, they're not enemies. The woman undresses, puts on that stupid paper gown they give you, but she's been tearing around, busy all day, she's superwoman, late for everything, she's sweaty, it's because of that damn synthetic underwear, so she digs through her purse and finds a tissue and wipes herself, a form of politeness, right? Then she hops on the table, ready or not, here I am, willing to be examined, a generic undertaking, doctor comes in, polite conversation, routine pelvic, she (the doctor) has been the woman's doctor for years, and she (the doctor), down at the end of the table, great presence of mind, asks suddenly, 'Are you sending yourself somewhere?'

"Get this. The woman has a postage stamp neatly affixed to her lower left-hand corner, incorrect you know, supposed to be the upper right-hand corner, and it's a federal offense to use government glue in a less than appropriate place, but obviously she had a postage stamp caught in that tissue she wiped herself with, and it's a good thing they both had a sense of humour."

"You are incorrigible," says the fictioneer. "What kind of story is that? It's an urban myth. A medical myth. A postal myth."

"Or a nursery rhyme?" says Buch. "It might be a nurse story but there's no romance. I suppose it's arguably a sexist story, since the woman is in an uncomfortable position. It could be a story about how we can send ourselves anywhere if we have the right postage. A story about the patriarchal stamp suddenly shifting con/text. A critical text about ways of conducting investigations. *Belle-lettres.*"

The fictioneer stuffs her fingers in her ears. "Stop. Enough already."

But Buch is relentless. "A text that pre-supposes sortage and delivery. An epistolary novel. An interrupted poem. A professional exam. A polemic against mailing. No – male/ing. An aerobics class: the pelvic tilt. A reading of the body of the body of language. It is, dear fictioneer, a ficto-criticism, a necessary departure from genre and its expectations. Pelvic or no, to de-genre requires surprise at what one finds in or on the text, that glorious moment when form cannot contain text and everything becomes *Buch*, a usurpation of expectation and critical stance. The physician/critic better hesitate to open this letter, because, innocent as it might be accidental, it contains an argument against any clear-cut genre."

"I quit," says the fictioneer. "I quit. I resign. I relinquish, I abandon my life to you."

"Oh, don't quit yet," says Hannike Buch. "We've only just begun. I need to finish Ruttowski's saga."

Narrendichtung/ Novelle/ Ode/ Oper, Operette/
Oratorium/ Ossianische Dichtung/ Parabel/ Parodie/
Pastoral/ Patriachade/Predigt/ Prosagedicht/ Rätsel/
Reportage/ Rhetorik/ Roman/ Romanze/ Saga/ Sage/
Satire/ Satyrspiel/ Schnaderhüpfel/ Schwank/ Science
Fiction/ Sonett/ Sprichwort, Spruch/ Tagebuch/
Tagelied/ Testament/ Theater/ Tierdichtung/
Totengespräch/ Tragikomödie/ Tragödie/ Utopie/
Witz/Zauberspruch, Gebet – (16)

Intervention: the Crime

In the transport they were allowed to take whatever they most wanted from their old lives, divided as those lives had been. They stood like upright anchovies in the huge moving vans that pulled together from the farthest circumference of the country, magnets in a spoked destination. They had been told they could bring refrigerators if they wanted. Expensive stereos, their favourite clothing, scotch tape even, if it made them feel happier to have the little cellophane rolls in their pockets. They could bring fishing tackle, baseball bats, Royal Doulton figurines even, although they were warned there was very little place for these things, and when one wit quoted the Margaret Atwood poem about fishhooks and open eyes he was removed. Forcibly.

Although they knew they would have no needs, that their physical necessities would be taken care of, everyone accepted the invitation to bring something, and they stood in the jouncing trucks with their duffle bags and their knapsacks, their Samsonite briefcases and even, yes, their battered old leather attachés. The ones who brought briefcases were clearly desperate for lost documents; a briefcase filled with canned ham and nylon stockings is a pathetic folio. Those who didn't understand looked longingly at them; those who did, looked punctiliously away.

Although they were permitted to laugh and joke in the trucks, they kept surprisingly quiet. It was crowded, but never packed so tightly that no one could sit down. Still, they stood, hands at their sides, half at invisible lecterns and half at invisible desks. Only a few railers demanded to know where they were going when the drivers lowered the back ramps to let them out for fresh air, bathroom breaks, for hamburgers and pop. And except for one character who kept demanding beer, after which he demanded frequent stops to take a leak, they were definitely too quiet.

They were transported to the fields, the wide yellow fields that stretch from the Rockies to the bottom of the basin. It was an unseasonably hot autumn, the frogs and mosquitoes pretending innocence. When they stood divided but together with their infinitely diminished possessions at the edge of the stubble, only then could they finally believe that they would not require the one thing they had been forbidden to bring: words.

It was a humane transportation. None of them was sick, and no one had died of fever. They were certain to be treated well, housed and fed, although there was no structure there on the edges of the great fields. One driver unloaded a big blue cooler and gestured toward the noisy critic: "Beer," he said. "Thirsty work out here." The bottles clinked.

To live in the fields of Alberta for the rest of your natural life. It sounded arcane, even antipodean, almost delightful, as though they were being given permission of a sort. But without words. Oh, conversation and telephone calls were allowed, but no books and no blank paper, and those who bothered to etch ink all over their bodies with forbidden ballpoints or who scratched letters on the wooden sides of the truck boxes soon discovered that the words went nowhere, were simply effaced by the steady wear of grain dust. They weren't particularly well guarded: their keepers were a happy-go-lucky Siksika tribe who encouraged them to go ahead and try to walk to Vancouver. They would simply be transported back to the fields and have to start the long journey over again. Enough to keep a person busy for a few years. And why leave? The fields were warm and relatively free; old longings proved disappointing. But they very soon divided into their old camps and took up their old animosities, the writers and the critics.

The critics ran the combines and the writers were in charge of the piles of grain. This separation made the critics imagine they occupied an elevated position – access to machinery made them feel important. But alone in their air-conditioned cabs, following the inexorable swaths around and around endless fields, they got lonely. The writers were having more fun on the ground. Three poets shovelled a pile of grain from one spot to another, impromptu performances took place. It was surprising how much the writers remembered of their own work. How much they liked to quote it, delicious malice in its re-articulation. The critics had trouble remembering their arguments and cross-references.

At night, they huddled together for warmth (they were issued parkas and caps, mitts, even high boots to avoid ankle stubble burn) there in the immense fields with the combines beating their stolid path around and around the swaths in the blue dusk. The whole flat of prairie from Gleichen to where Calgary had been and on up to the mountains held itself under a grain dust *chador*, the chaff high and sweet in the blueing air and the combines making their unswervable path past the lamp globes of the patient trucks. They knew there was no smell so fragrant, no dust so prickly, and their bodies thrummed with the combines in the dusk's heart. On the green edge of the sun's last light, the mountains creased the sky with an absolute and unblurred edge. And while the prairie elephants beat, beat, beat, their sullen path, they stood in the groundgauze of chaff and breathed deep another winnowing.

Just as there were no words, there were no granaries, and the high cones of oats and wheat and barley became the writers' playground. They dived into the slippery golden slopes, slid down the piles on toboggans. The critics began to yell at the writers from their elevated combines, ordering them to stop disarranging the piles, to work seriously. But the writers laughed and insisted that the piles looked better disarranged, that the grain needed to be spread around. There was plenty of wheat gum, always plenty of healthy exercise, and words enough spoken into the sound of the crisp elusive air. There were those who claimed they were writing the great transportation novel on the backs of beer labels, but although they may have begun, the greater rhythms of shovelling and dreaming and sleeping seduced them, their feet moving over the insubstantial ground of gauzy dust while the mountains in the distance grew sharper and sharper. Grey fieldmice chewed up the beer labels.

The food was monotonous but good: beer, fresh corn on the cob, sausages and apricots. Too much like Germany, complained the noisy critic, until a writer reminded him that Germans don't generally eat either corn or apricots, that he was forgetting his references.

There were those who resented their exile to the fields, claimed to be allergic to grain dust, claimed for themselves exemption or an early and inevitable grave. But curiously, they failed to cough and choke, to swell up; and no one died.

Even if they fought, everyone seemed to breathe more freely than when they had inhaled the dust of words and books. And although they moved with a peculiar stubble walk and ran a swathjumper's run, their bodies, male and female, felt easier than ever before. The loose heaps of combined straw were a lover's delight, and sometimes the cries of passion that thinned the air seemed to rival the beating of the elephant combines. Transportation grew accustoming and although they knew their literary history, knew they were supposed to be suffering terrible hardship, they had trouble formulating themselves a persecution. In short, they felt relieved, but dared only to examine that relief secretly. They sparred openly, verbally, the writers and the critics insisting that each side was more correct, though none would take the blame for their transportation.

But something or someone always trades a story in. It might have been the deepening twilights. It might have been the wash of dust that clung and moved suggestively past the hollows of the ground. It might have been when the writers began to burn the piles of grain. Of course they had matches, of course they could burn the grain, for once the world was not hungry. The cones of grain became art, pyres of colour, sometimes small explosions leaping to a slide of flame. The grain fires burned dangerously beautiful: the word-people held out their hands to warm, joined other hands to dance around the fires, and listened to the hiss and spit of kernels. And then, on a given midnight when the writers sat together around one small fire's circumference, a woman's voice began to speak in a way that made everyone shiver. This is what she said: "In the transport they were allowed to take whatever they most wanted. . . They stood like upright anchovies. . ."

"Wait," a voice approached from the yellow dark outside the fire's light. "Anchovies?"

Silence. The elephants had stopped beating – it was too tough to combine. It was three o'clock in the morning and while the grain fires melted, the critics had come in.

"That's not a good simile," said the voice, and the fire's genred circumference seemed suddenly smaller and colder, divisive and closured.

They had taken sides, divided themselves into the genres of their own exile.

2. Footnotes on the edge of nowhere

"A genre is less like a game than like a code of social behaviour."
     E.D. Hirsch, *Validity in Interpretation*

". . .those cumbersome differences of cases, genders, moods, and tenses, which I think, was a piece of a Tower of Babel's curse. . ."
     Sir Philip Sydney, *Apologia Poetica*

          The cryptic subversions of ficto-criticism demand that all structures (and their arguments) be broken into through the inevitable weak point of the basement window. The basement window of the generic house of criticism is the footnote, lurking at the bottom of the text, under the page, at the back of all arguments; the footnote's positioning shouts inviolability, furnishes an argument with authority, declaims its own superiority. All else is opinion, but the footnote is sacrosanct, contains the real declension of argument: genuine recognitions, quiet political nods, even extended ramblings, but with an authority that the body does not hold. Footnotes jostle each other's elbows but manage to live together without connection, yet enact intertext (Kroetsch, *Labyrinths* 17). They are a seemingly random but ordered (and certainly numbered) troop, ready to come riding to the rescue in the form of a backup buchaneer.

And footnotes lurk at the bottom of every text.

Presuming that the ineffable flavour of a definite article is missing, you are immediately confronted with the noun of footnote. See here, footnote asserts, I'm going to offer you some research, an explanation or two, a comment on the text (we're going to have to find a different word for text, *magic* perhaps, or *net*, a series of holes held together by string), but footnotes make a claim, say, "I will provide you with my background, my pedigree,

my certificate of health and my family inclination." Not even a
footnote yet, and look at where you are. (Although a footnote
might be necessary for the next word – a lovely verb – "lurk.") The
lurk in text is recognizable, its sinister bending, its furtive
scratchings and truculent ambushes. But the fact is, when your
footnotes lurk, dear buchaneer, your text might be in trouble,
probably sabotaged from within, through the necessary outsiders,
although not necessarily troublemakers, of footnotes.

Footnotes lurk at the bottom of the text. Lurkage is one thing,
but the text is not a pail, full or empty, water or milk or chop (all of
which the fictioneer has carried plenty five-gallon heaviness of), it
sounds more like something that is to blame for something else.
"I'll get to the bottom of this," the buchaneer says to her teenage
daughter, who is smarter than she is and has learned *how* to use
footnotes; she learned in grade eight, and the buchaneer never
has. The day they were taught she was home sick with the flu,
playing hooky, but god forbid that should be her excuse for not
knowing how to footnote a footnote, or how to build one. They are
a sophisticated strategy, and not to be ignored. And although
speculations on the bottoms of things are endlessly possible, the
bottom line, so to speak, the lowest part, the fundamental quality,
the empty glass, the buchaneer has to move on, to what is *under*
the page.

Now this too is ambiguous, and certainly needs a little further
discussion, ahem, deferred pleasure. "Under the page"? These
pages are white, printed back to back, one page lies neatly under
another, and under them a desk or perhaps a lectern, which
fascinates the buchaneer because it has migrated from churches
and their services, and what does that say about buchaneers and
what they do in lecture rooms, but also because lectern is close to
lecher and thus gives her a chance to check on all lewdness and
prurience, to roll around in *lickerous* for a while. But she is going
too far, footnoting the footnotes, she hasn't even gotten to the end

of the first sentence of her initial contention of the second part of
the "Fictioneer as Ficto-Critic," despite the crime of intervention,
and although she struggles valiantly, she hasn't yet succumbed to
that little number at the bottom of the page. Which is not quite the
same as the bottom of the text, but will have to do for now.
Page/text aren't interchangeable, and she wants to return to what's
under the page, with its suggestion of layers, ranking,
concealment.

She (buchaneer? fictioneer?) writes this stuff, whatever you
might call it, under concealment, an assumed name, a name with
its own peculiar history, that she unearthed or took on seven,
maybe eight years ago, when she was invaded by ficto-criticism.
She has to be careful about spoiling her fictional reputation, no get
that straight, her fiction's reputation. The truth is, fiction doesn't
want fictioneers committing infidelities with other forms.

She was – on that historic occasion – in Stavanger, Norway, at
an International Arts Festival, giving a reading, giving a talk,
making ficto-criticism, and sneaking out at night to listen to the
festival's best imported American jazz, having to sneak out under
the disapproving eyes of the hotel porter. There was a chubby little
Norwegian writer following her around, he was scared shitless, but
determined. He wanted to sleep with a Canadian writer. Does this
sound familiar? Does this explain an earlier fictional inscription? Is
this a footnote to the other story of the war between buchaneer
and fictioneer, of the transportation quarrel between writer and
critic? Or is it pre/text, despite its placement in this text, and the
other a footnote for this recounting?

Nothing could deter her when she wanted to hear jazz, and she
listened intently, sitting next to a writer whose books, she was
embarrassed to say, she had not yet read. Although he was not old,
he walked with a cane; and although he was not old, his hair was
salt and pepper (does this image require a footnote?), and he was
in the despicable habit of smoking thick smelly cigars. All of which

she was willing to forgive for his eyes, which had an undescribable and extraordinary intensity, quite enough to make her cross her legs in perturbation. The saxophone grieved with that rough-sided, tongue-licking asphalt layer that goes through your bones, so she didn't hear his name. Actually, she refused to believe that anyone had mentioned his name; as long as she didn't hear it, he hadn't been introduced, in life or in text, but (and this is a stage whisper, not a footnote) she knew she was in trouble.

So they spent the evening staring at each other past the music. And the next day, without further footnote, they were introduced, and this time, no saxophone, no grumble of other voices, she had no choice but to hear his name. He smiled at her and repeated himself. "Buch," he said. "I am very pleased to meet you. We enjoyed the same text last night."

She stared at him. "What?" (The old Canadian vernacular, a shoelace that will trip itself anywhere in the world.)

"Buch," he said softly. "Imagine being born a Buch."

She was again[1] struck dumb in front of five or six people, and she stammered the truth, she is continually stammering the truth. "I envy your name," she said. Imagine, she thought, *being born a Buch.*

He laughed. "Yes," he said.

She whispered it this time. "I wish I had your name."

And one of the five or six observers, the notetakers, the starfuckers, the sycophants and advisors, offered, "You could marry him."

Buch only smiled, as if he had heard that line before.

And the wedding, which celebration became a footnote to the earlier event, had the wonderful cachet of a previously inflected desire and its fulfillment, had the ring of authenticity. There was still a search for an official who could perform the ceremony, since she still did not speak German and he had not learned Dutch, and neither of them had even attempted Norwegian. Finally, someone (a woman it was, the mayor perhaps or a retired opera singer) was discovered, and the fictioneer received official permission, along with the necessary documentation (all properly footnoted) to name herself Hannike Buch.

Usage is the real test of a footnote, and Hannike Buch publishes crypto-fiction left and right and never centre, she can't be shut down. And although you might vociferously demand if not a footnote at least a hint of whether or not that peculiar conjunction was ever consummated, you will have to watch for the secret citation on the edge of another nowhere, under another text. Suffice to say that Buch, he of the enviable name, is a fine German novelist, and *The Wedding at Port-au-Prince* was produced long before their presumably footnoted exchange, and it has nothing whatsoever to do with Stavanger.

But Hannike Buch is out there, with her toughness and resilience; she is her own genre, she sets her own priorities. If she goes back to the beginning of this exegesis, she discovers she has not even progressed past the footnotes lurking at the bottom of the page, under the text, behind all arguments. Or under the page, at the backs of all arguments. Behind the backs of all arguments. She hasn't touched that yet, the resonant possibilities of backs, a secret treachery to them that goes back to Julius Ceasar and farther even, backing out, backing away, a backdrop. The backs of arguments are narrow and rigid, the ladder of the spine a vulnerable curve: arguments contain all potential for backache, backfiring. Against arguments, their rat-a-tat-tat, their reasonable quarrelsomeness. But this has gone too far. She is enmired in her own absent footnotes. Let her go back to the beginning.

She pretends now to abhor footnotes of any kind: bottom notes, end notes, side notes. While notes in music make perfect sense, perfect pitch, in criticism they enact a strange ensnarement of the text, effect breakage, the smug intrusion of those little numbers citing their own importance. Oh, she uses them. They proclaim the extent of her knowledge, how many critics she has been tempted to appropriate. At the same time, they destroy the aesthetic page, which for the fictioneer, though not quite for Hannike Buch, is a blocky fictional page, flawless, continuous. "The result of all this. . . footnoting and appendix-noting is that the volume has a most chaotic and bewildering look." (This is the O.E.D. footnoting its own definition.)

There are some who would argue that a footnoted page offers its own aesthetic, but she is not one of those. She reads along, happily enough, whether Said or Hutcheon or Eagleton or Cixous, and there's that admonishing little number, shaking its finger at her, telling her to go back, check the reference, the source. Strange how mystical language delineates critical vocabulary. The source of sources: an originator, a creator. These notes overwrite a palimpsest of insecurity, someone else has always said it first or said it better, and thus the buchaneer's terror of plagiarism is really an inside-out terror of originality.

Yes, you can get her on that one, the romance of originality, such an old story fictioneers tell, nothing new (not footnoted anyway) under the sun, but at least, goddamn it, some good, honest stealing, and without the footnote of Faulkner's famous, "I make my living telling lies." The buchaneer contends that Faulkner defined his genre for himself. He was happy to offer poetry, song, story, maps, lists, even dates, and call them all lies, although having survived him, buchaneers insist on the nomenclature of lies as fiction. (And, reader, you thought all that talk about her assumed name was a digression.)

But if footnotes are vicious traps snapping at the legs of the reader bounding across the page, genre is the coffin that contains form. It might have something to do with biology, the species of buchaneers, whether they have antlers or that famous flat tail. If Hannike Buch were a conscientious critic, she would insert a neat little footnote here citing Margaret Atwood's *Survival*, giving you the low-down on beavers and the deaths of innocent animals (victims, right?), but she refuses. Genre is an act of nomenclature too, a designation, even though (and here's a footnote), the root of the conception of genre seems to be the relation of the literary work to its audience (check Frye for this, and Aristotle too). This relation has been pretty much effaced. The audience, now, appears to have damn little effect on genre, which is presented as a given. Readers are forced to read the text through its label, its designated destination, a product rather than a process. Despite Todorov maintaining the importance of not product but the act of reading as a "mode of construction" (39). And don't assume this is a footnote; it's just a random page number.

And here's another double-whammy to the fictioneer, a real Frye (Northrop) for you, sweet reason itself. "The object of making these distinctions in literary tradition is not simply to classify, but to judge authors in terms of the conventions they themselves chose" (209). One might as well be a bizarre and extinct species, given the frygidity [sic] of this formaldehyde bottle. The object of making these distinctions is not *simply* (emphasis Buch's) to classify, but *first of all* to classify, that act of not only division and arrangement but restriction, a danger to the nation if the enemy gets its hands on this secret weapon: the enemy is always the fictioneer, the nation always the buchaneer. But worse than division and arrangement, judgment: "to judge *authors* in terms of the conventions they themselves chose." To judge authors living or dead, under real or assumed names, not texts, hah, that would demand an act of *reading*, and, furthermore, to stick it to them twice by judging them in terms of the conventions they themselves choose. Authors, and even Hannike Buch will back the fictioneer up on this one, do not choose conventions. They struggle, they flail, against them. Every convention is a coffin the author attempts to escape from, a Houdini act that beggars words. Eli Mandel says it more brilliantly than ever she can.

Houdini

I suspect he knew that trunks are metaphors,
could distinguish between the finest rhythms
unrolled on rope or singing in a chain
and knew the metrics of the deepest pools

I think of him listening to the words
spoken by manacles, cells, handcuffs,
chests, hampers, roll-top desks, vaults,
especially the deep words spoken by coffins

escape, escape: quaint Harry in his suit
his chains, his desk, attached to all attachments
how he'd sweat in that precise struggle
with those binding words, wrapped around him
like that mannered style, his formal suit

and spoken when? by whom? What thing first said
"there's no way out?"; so that he'd free himself,
leap, squirm, no matter how, to chain himself again,
once more jump out of the deep alive
with all his chains singing around his feet
like the bound crowds who sigh, who sigh. (70)

Mandel does not use the word genre but he might as well have.
Houdini's struggle is the artist's struggle to escape that coffin of
convention, named by form and policed by genre. The fictioneer is
forced to chain herself again and again in order to break those
chains, to subvert coffin and convention. If there are buchaneers in
Mandel's poem, they are part of the "bound crowds."

If she adopts this Frygian position of evaluating a text through its
bondage, buchaneer reads herself a sado-masochistic literature

and criticism, no matter which genre is chosen as victim (another Atwood footnote here). For the limitations of genre definition negate the creative possibilities incited by the friction of the text within its category. Michael Ondaatje's *In the Skin of a Lion* proclaims itself, loud and clear on the dust jacket, right under the title (and it is not a footnote), a novel; instead of using that implied adherence to convention as a moment of departure and a subversive act, critics have wasted both words and footnotes trying to prove that *In the Skin of a Lion* is *not* a novel. This disapproval is not reading, not even buchaneering, but assembly line sorting (which bolt goes in which hole?).

Buch takes both comfort and refuge in Maurice Blanchot: "The book is the only thing that matters, the book as it is, far from genres, outside of the categorical subdivisions – prose, poetry, novel, document – in which it refuses to lodge and to which it denies the power of establishing its place and determining its form. A book no longer belongs to a genre; every book stems from literature alone. . ." (136). When what becomes important is not the process of reading, but assigning genre as product, you are about to commit much the same distinctions as people who wish to have only sons and thus kill girl-babies. Literature that refuses to be categorized will continue to appear, but when it is badly read, unlovingly welcomed, you are in danger of un/reading what might be the best of our writing. This touching critical attachment for the coffin of convention is emphatically a tool of the dominant patriarchal and pedantic literary tradition, the same one that insists, over and over again, that the canon consists primarily of poetry by white European males.

And so, fictioneer or buchaneer, we have no choice but to become Houdinis, to use the chains that bind the text as metaphors, to escape all determiners' coffins, to break the laws of Frye et. al., to subvert definition. Which is where fictioneer arrives at ficto-criticism, that version of writing practised by her revisionist friend, Hannike Buch, who has been doubly introduced and footnoted. If she were forced to define this strange hybridization in terms of accepted critical terminology, she might seize upon that wonderful term, *bricolage*, "conceived by Lévi-Strauss as a concept and critical strategy directed against his own historical-philosophical tradition, one which attempts to use pragmatically the concepts and tools of analysis of the tradition but in a way which avoids its ideological limitations and assumptions" (Carroll 164). David Carroll is the critic, here discussing Lévi-Strauss, but Buch is damned if she can find her own reference to him. Does she dare to leave him, dangling there? Of course, these stories Hannike Buch substitutes for criticism are not neutral instruments at all, she would never pretend they are. The distinction between the writer and the critic, which Carroll's *The Subject in Question* asserts is becoming less and less pertinent, is nevertheless a distinction that is maintained, especially by buchaneers. If metafiction contains its own self-aware analysis (check Linda Hutcheon, *Narcissitic Narrative: the metafictional paradox* 1), then what is left for the critic to undertake? The fictioneer usurps/intervents the buchaneer's sacred role. Or is it the other way around? This usurpation is now a regular occurrence, and however much she may like or dislike its implied narcissism, she must admit that the fictional text is encroaching on the critical text. By a curious extension of this development, it is arguable that the most interesting critics at work in Canada today are themselves – Frye's term – authors and poets *first*. So, what then, to do, if one is a critic, if one has conventions – excuse her – standards? Hannike Buch gives free advice: write fiction.

Hannike Buch writes ficto-criticism, cryptic and full of friction. As criticism it does everything wrong, as fiction it does nothing right. Of all forms, criticism is the one most frozen in its (as Frye would have it) sub-genre: "there is a broad distinction between works of FICTION (e.g., the novel) and thematic works (e.g., the essay)" (209). (Where these page numbers come from Hannike Buch does not know – they simply appear, she has no footnotes to back them up.) But Frye's e.g.'s are killing. Criticism, too, is damned by its category, its conventions, must return to footnotes, their irrevocable interference, their own implied displeasure with the text, a *coitus interruptus* of idea. It seems strange to hear buchaneers so nervous about the narcissism of metafiction when in fact, criticism is backing itself into footnotal *mise en abyme*, an endless duplication of mirror-after-critical-mirror held up in order to ensure the convention of form, in order to avoid the lie, the guess, the leap forward into theft. And every footnote is a nail in the coffin of criticism.

∽ ∽

The fictioneer was driving down the street in her old and rusty Porsche. She needed a new one, but that was out of the question. The best she had been able to do was get herself a new name, which she tried on once in a while to see how well it fit. She loved its doubleness, its ambiguity, another language, another signifier. Buch, she would say quietly, at the library borrowing books, in bookstores when she demanded a written receipt. Nobody turned a hair, nobody noticed. She was merely a customer, safe in Canada, where no one understood *buch*, and where foreign names are a dime-store-novel a dozen. She wrote criticism, but they couldn't know that – it was a dying and subsidiary genre in an intellectual ghetto. How were they to know that she wrote criticism in order to exist, that by acting as critic she was able to project herself as fictional character far more easily than as writer? – although she shared the same motivation, the commonplace that all writers are inspired by passion, a passion for words, pure and simple. She knew about passion all right.

So just as she drove down the street, sticking to her own lane, careful to keep herself parallel to the traffic on either side, she wrote crypto-fiction. After reading a text, fiction or not, she would write a parallel text, a story or not a story that was ficto-commentary on the fiction she was supposed to "elucidate." She liked that signifier, thought of it as a lightbulb, and that was pretty much the way her ficto-criticism worked, like a very bright hundred-watt bulb suddenly flicked on in the room of a book. There were no footnotes, which distressed everyone. Instead, there were long meanderings and stories and denials and harangues and poetry and repetitions and exaggerations and ignorings and sometimes even drunkenness caught in those ficto-criticisms. She was trying to avoid plot. She was trying to avoid position, she was trying to avoid form, although she could not, of course, avoid either rhetoric or sex. There was a concerted effort to impose on her the label of autobiography (or of biotext), but she just laughed, and turned herself back into her alter ego. Her alter ego the buchaneer.

The Porsche was like a page, she could feel it under her hands, could not stop it from running away with her. Speeding up, like words when the eye follows them in a swift race, undeniable. And then, a half-ton truck pulled out in front of her. A pick-up, as they say in Alberta, although that signifier has more than one signification. In the back of the pick-up was a coffin, a beautifully burnished mahogany and brass-handled coffin, riding along in understated elegance, on its way to some rodeo or another (it couldn't possibly be going to a funeral), a germinal or mythological event, a source. The pick-up had the usual bumper stickers (*I'd rather push this beast a mile than buy from Petro-Can*), the usual gun-rack, the usual two heads close together on the left side: what you'd expect in Calgary. Hannike Buch followed that pick-up. It was easy, she just gave the Porsche its nose, and there they were, weaving in and out of traffic with wonderful ease. Speeding up, slowing down, that coffin riding as dignified and determined as a librarian. When they reached the outskirts, Hannike Buch pulled up beside the truck, waved at the handsome young man driving (and of course he had sideburns), "pull over, pull over." He frowned, then caught on and bumped to the shoulder.

She walked up to his window like a mountie. "Hey, what have you got in the back?"

He looked down at her from his window. "What?"

"That – " she gestured with her thumb. She couldn't say the word.

But he wasn't too shy to talk back. "What's it to you? Good for putting stuff in."

Even Hannike Buch believes in language. "But it's a *coffin*."

"A what?"

"A coffin."

He scratched his chin, then opened his door and swung down. "Wanna see it?" The head beside him stayed in the cab.

Of course, thought Hannike Buch, that's what I wanted, to see. He gave her a hand up over the tailgate and opened the brass hasps, swung the lid back, gestured proudly. "There."

It was empty.

"Nice, eh," said the cowboy, running a thumb and forefinger along the velvet-lined edge. "Gonna put my – "

"Don't tell me," said Hannike Buch, "just don't tell me." She jumped down from the truck, climbed into her car, and spun a U-turn.

I hope you don't expect a moral to this story. There is none. No footnotes either. Well, maybe one.

[1](again)

Extrapolations from Miracles [1]

Out of Carol Shields

I thought I might have to put everyone in a large feather bed, you know the kind, European in origin, four-poster certainly, if not canopied, with a quilt as light and thick as an icing. They would cavort there, under cover, in a separate and secret language of finger and toe, belly and knee, having jumped the fencing pages of fiction to come together, out of miracles into another miracle, characters sprung from story but storied so well they carry their stories with them into this huge and collective bed where they tumble and roil. Of course, this *couvade* would be just that, a *couvade*; they would refuse to let their language measure them such limitation and the bed would be a moment only, temporary. They would romance their slippers and knot the sashes of sky-blue dressing gowns, order coffee and croissants, telephone their mothers, crawl under the bed (lots of room there) in search of a sock or a newspaper and pull out a trumpet and a bag of sea salt. Certainly never interact properly, with the discernment and dignity expected of characters conjured from the same book. They would name the book arbitrary, having been bound and glued and covered by it, a certain number of stories and characters assigned to this edition of miracles, but more, infinitely more, possible. Probable, if you'll permit.

Instead, they've insisted on taking the bus, they've all grabbed a seat on the "Pardon" bus waiting out that Winnipeg deluge pulled over to the side of the road because the windshield wipers can't keep up. They are all versions of Carol Shields' *Various Miracles*, but they do not know that. They are happy on that stranded bus, unaware that everyone else is also charactered in the miracle cycle, unaware that they themselves are characters. The rain is shouting on the roof, but inside it is curiously quiet and contained, despite their festive talk, the singsong at the back. Imagine that. Winnipeg is a good place to be stuck on a bus in a rainstorm. You can be stranded for a reasonably long time, with enough food and good reading to last, Canadian reserve giving way to a generosity and pleasure beneath the frost. And everyone from the periphery of *Miracles* is there.

Roger has found a treat for dinner, a beautifully precise leg of fresh spring lamb that he will roast for Helene and her mother after rubbing it with basil and thyme. They've only been back from France a week and their reunion (the reunion of Roger and Helene's mother, and even Roger and Helene) has been ecstatic; they cannot imagine how they lasted the year apart, and now Roger kisses Helene's mother shamelessly, rubs her buttocks with his hands, even when Helene is around. She'll have to get used to it, says Helene's mother cheerfully. France has taught her a thing or two. Roger wonders if there is mint in the cupboard, for Helene and her mother's kitchen is deplorably stocked. He will do something about that soon, Roger, he imagines rows of neat spice bottles lining the shelf above the stove, fresh herbs growing on the apartment balcony. He feels the package with his hand, checks to make sure the meat is not leaking onto his neatly pressed pants. One corner of the paper is getting a bit soggy, he's surprised the butcher didn't wrap it better, but then he thinks of the smell of the roasting lamb, and a quiet smile creeps across his face. It's a smile that makes the woman sitting next to him want to put her hand on his arm. She has never had a man cook lamb, or much else for that matter, for her. Her husband sometimes made her a pot of tea, or brought her toast in bed on Mother's Day. In the early years, that was. But then he got all taken up with his writing, his poetry, his writing, his poetry, and how his teaching and his children and his wife and his job and the climate and having to get the oil in the car changed interfered with his real mission in life, the words in his notebooks. Those notebooks made her resentful, she'd begun to neglect the ironing and shun the vacuum cleaner, even though as a Professor's wife she didn't really have to do the cleaning herself, she could have hired someone. But she refused, she insisted on doing it but did not do it, knew it was driving him crazy, making him stiff and fierce with resentment. She waited for him to give her a sign, to recognize her refusals. A paper cone of flowers would have been enough, a spool of brightly-coloured thread, if he'd offered spontaneously, beyond the rigidities of Christmas and her birthday, pulled it out of his pocket and said, "Here, I found this for you." She would have wept and cleaned energetically, done the windows with vinegar and newspaper, polished every finger-printed surface to a high mirror. But he didn't, and even in the divorce proceedings, she waited in vain for a mention of her desperate slovenliness, her chaotic keeping of their house. Instead, he kept his face immobile and his lips pressed together when the judge cited mutual incompatibility. And all the difficulties he enumerates now in his poems – domestic breakup poems – are abstractions, errors of the soul, not the real cause: sticky floors and mouldy taps. And here she is in Winnipeg – Winnipeg! Winnipeg hadn't existed before her divorce. She didn't know what to do with her alimony, and decided, now that it is really too late, to go back to school. But she couldn't go to college at home: her husband's latest book has made him mildly famous and people insist on asking if she is related to him. Here, people read Canadian poetry and there is a good school of weather fluctuation, which she has decided to study. It is lovely, sitting on a bus stranded by a weather fluctuation, next to a neat man holding a rather lumpish parcel and smiling to himself. She thinks she might become a Canadian citizen, if they'll permit her; she thinks of getting a job in a weather station in northern Manitoba, keeping records of temperature and rainfall. The temperature inside this bus is perfect, cool enough so that people feel happy in their sweaters, but warm enough so that no one shivers, despite the curtain of rain that separates them from the actual world. The immigrant man sitting in the second seat from the front is relieved about that. He is inordinately troubled by temperature, he has a recurring dream in which he is in charge of microphones and tape-recorders at a huge international conference, and because of something that he does or omits doing, the world gets hotter and hotter. It is a nightmare of heat and he is responsible; somehow, through his job, if he only does the right thing, he can reverse this terrible heat. He flies frantically from lectern to control panel, he taps at beehive microphones, plugs this appliance in and unplugs that, and the world gets hotter. He knows there is one action, one gesture that will resolve this nightmare, but he has never been able to determine what it is, and so he always pulls that plug accidentally from its socket. His wife blames his dream on central heating, the fact that Canadians sleep in rooms far too warm for sleeping, but even if he flings wide a window in the dark of January, the dream persists. He tells it again and again to his wife and children, in the language of home, their round dark eyes around the breakfast table watching him as he mops his brow and recounts the intensity of the heat. His eldest daughter blames the northern winter and thinks it is a transference of longing on his part, because they emigrated from a much warmer country, but she does not say this. She is determined to forget the language they arrived with, she will speak only English, although in a few years she will learn French too. But she does not know her linguistic capacity yet, and so she is impatient with her swarthy father, his wide gesturing arms and his voluable torrent of angst, his suspicion of anything electrical. He wants everything to be made of glass or wood and he refuses to consider buying a microwave, which all her friends use to heat their after-school pizzas. He passes his hand over surfaces with great suspicion, checking for non-metallic realism. He does not know that the man on the bus across the aisle from him is a salesman in natural substances, marble and tourmaline, sea grass and cane, rough cottons and silky wools. The salesman works for a company determined to out-compete synthetics, that advertises itself to those people who refuse to allow anything artificial in their *lifestyles*. That is the language used in the company ads, placed in ecology magazines and architectural design features. He knows that the language is unfairly loaded, that it caters to a lingering belief in the naturalness of the natural, but ever since 1974, when he was on a plane forced to make an emergency landing in a barley field, he has somehow believed it too. After jumping down the inflatable slide, they found themselves in the middle of a sea of golden and bearded stalks, bending ever so gently in front of a gentle breeze, a much more suitable landing cushion than the hard, marked grey of the airport's tarmac. It might have been the barley and its rather prickly texture reminding him of heavy woven cotton from the Andes – no, he must have been thinking of llama's wool, but anyway, that particular wheaty colour – the feel of the barley heads as he brushed across their tops, standing well back from the airplane, hand in hand, he and the woman who had been sitting next to him, Frances her name was, that made him decide to rely on the natural world alone. One quick and daring landing enough to persuade him that the act of sitting in the big belly of a plane, held up by ridiculously flimsy wings, was an unnatural one. Now he carries a big double case with swatches of rough-woven cloth, little square sample tiles of natural stone. He enjoys the rainstorm because it is making him late; he feels that being always on time is unnatural, that we should move by darkness and light rather than by hour and minute. At this moment, he is delighted to be poised between the dark cloudburst and the afternoon. He lays his case across his lap and props his elbows on it, hearing the rain on the roof of the bus as though it were water over stone. His calmness has a good effect on the passengers behind him, who are nothing less than terrified. They are here on vacation, a vacation intended to make them forget their son's untimely death, by a motorcycle accident in France, a death which they cannot forget and which they relive again and again in their imaginations, the skid of the wheeled machine and then the bounce and sprawl and shatter of the child who was theirs, bone and flesh and body impacted too much for human fragility. They had to identify his body, still covered in plaster, had to be there when it arrived at Dover, his face as chalk as the cliffs. They have taken a vacation to forget, but they are reminded again and again: by every motorcycle on the street, by every young man swinging into a car, and now by the rain, the rain that is nothing like English rain, misty and persistent, but sudden and violent, an outburst so demanding and apocalyptic that the very bus they are on has to pull over and wait. The wife begins to cry, holding an edged handkerchief to her face and hoping she will not be noticed. The husband pats her knee, all he can do, for he is ready to cry as well, angry that they are here in a strange country, visiting his brother who was determined to leave Sheffield and immigrated after the war to this oddly flat city full of eastern Europeans and Mennonites. Yet, there is something different about this crying, here in Canada, awash with homesickness and regret and grief, for the cloudburst above seems to weep for them, thunderously, with a passion they feel but have tried to restrain. And they are certainly noticed: a young man several seats back comes stumbling forward, offers a small packet of tissues, although they can hardly understand him for the combination of his Canadian accent and his lisp. He is comforting in his size and his clumsiness, so unlike the grace they have bestowed on their own lost and now free to be perfect child. Unknowingly, they have a tenuous connection to the natural substances salesman in front of them. Had their son not stopped to indulge his geological interest, to look at a sandstone cliff unusual in formation, he would have missed the swerving truck by a good ten minutes. Nor can they know that sandstone walls are the latest in interior decorating. So they are grateful to the gawky young man who does what all kind-hearted and tender Canadians do – he talks and talks until they sniff and cheer up with listening, with being forced to listen. The lisping giant tells them that he studied at Oxford, that his thesis on Wittgenstein was subverted by his interest in French, and so they tell him about France, how their son was killed there in an accident, he gives them an excuse to speak their unspeakable grief, and he is wonderfully comforting in his clumsy listening, half-kneeling in the aisle of the bus which is sitting at the side of the road, waiting for the rain to stop. And in all their talk of France, none of them knows that a woman half-way back, quietly bent over a thickish book, is a follower of, an expert on, French feminist theory. She is married to a theologian, and it is this conjunction that has made her an expert on French feminism, that unbearable constant rub against someone imbued with knowledge, spilling over with information, about theology. French feminist theory, unlike the clouded and muddy allegories of Christianity, seems to her crisp and prism-like, a movement forward in language and idea, while theology flounders in its old conundrums, tries to untangle itself from what it was and what it is afraid to become. She tolerates her husband's theology, she with her head down, close to the page, she even revels in it sometimes, like she is capable of revelling in her husband's unexpected gas pains, so that she frequently cooks chili, but she won't put up with theology imposing sexism on her life, she won't stand for that. Last night he came home from a dinner in honour of a prominent British scholar passing through Winnipeg on a Canadian lecture tour and began talking about Lot's wife (Lot's wife indeed, as if she hadn't an identity of her own – that's the trouble with the Bible), mumbling about salt, why was she turned into a pillar of salt rather than sandstone. Dear God and Julia Kristeva. Concerned about salt when the real issue was Lot's wife, whose name was probably Caroline or Roberta (and here she actually smiled to herself, so unlikely did that sound), immobilized, stopped in her tracks, a male allegory, a male punishment if she'd ever heard of one. "I can't begin to tell you why she was turned into salt," she said determinedly, "but I can certainly speculate on why she looked back instead of trudging forward with that old lecher, Lot." Her husband's ears turned pink and he knotted his pajama pants very carefully. She sat up in bed, where she had been reading, propped against the pillows, and said even more determinedly, "She was sick of her lot in life." Delighted with this solution, she gave a little bounce, making the mattress jiggle, and couldn't resist repeating herself. "She was sick of her lot in life!" The phrase made her so impetuous that when her husband slid in next to her and turned off the lamp, she immediately unknotted his pajama pants and they left the discussion right there, with her lying on top of him in her favourite position, moving against his body very slowly and quietly. And now, sitting on that bus stopped in its tracks, knowing that she has hundreds of wonderfully thick French feminist texts to read, but that she can still unknot those old pajama pants, she is so happy she could sing. And someone else is singing, not just the group at the back of the bus, extemporizing on "Singing in the Rain," but a woman a few seats over, who hums under her breath while she reads a musical score. She is certainly memorizing a part, for she follows the notes and the words carefully. She wears a red coat, a little heavy for the season, but she is from Toronto and Torontonians always expect Winnipeg to be cold. She is beautiful, a beauty curiously located in the bridge of her nose, and it happens that she is the actress with the lead role in David Arnason's new musical. She has been out of work for some time, and this play is her chance to establish a reputation, to show the world her talent. She hopes that it will do well, that it will go farther than Winnipeg, and that she will go too. So with joy and dedication, and not just because print is her way of entering and escaping the world, she bends her head above her script, her score, memorizing the words she hopes will make her immortal. And although she is just getting to know Winnipeg, and although she has not yet read the stories of Carol Shields, she will, she most certainly will. You see the way that fictional miracles compound themselves?

For the real miracle is language, that we humans want not only to touch each other but that we want to exchange words, like marbles from a fist, that we want to hear discernible sounds from each other's mouths, that we want to decipher them, that we utter our own sounds and others understand them. Even more miraculous, that we put these various marks on paper, written or printed or typed, and others understand the message, make some connection with these peculiar runes. This is a sweet and terrifying exchange, this intricate and shared knowledge of what is certainly a secret code.

Why are we so seldom awed at the magic of these black marks, the heavy shape of words in our mouths, pebbles smoothed by the seas of articulation? These small gestures are punctuators, stops and starts, hesitations and implications. Who could have imagined that such scratches could conduct so much? A miracle, the miracle of language, a recognition that the real miracle is that there are miracles, themselves miraculous. Carol Shields knows this: she writes with one eye on the miracle of language and another on the miracle of miracles. Her stories excite their own awe. More than acts in the godgame of creation, they are small carvings of narrative reflection, beyond lie and legend, beyond plot and composition, allegation into miracle. For Carol Shields, the world is that moment when we bend to the blown page, and in reading discover a page from the story of ourselves, that coalesced moment when a complete stranger surprises us through an act of intimacy.

I have an image of Carol Shields, unsubstantiated of course, not real but fictional. She is wearing a buttercup yellow dress, floating and diaphanous. Underneath, her skin too is luminous, you can see through to her bones, which are also transparent, so that she seems almost a textured hologram, although not insubstantial, curiously tough, resilient. She has a wordnet in her hand, its fine mesh much different from any butterfly catcher, and she is sweeping the air in great delicate strokes, shaking the net empty into her lap and sweeping again in a semaphore at once determined and elegant. This is not the real Carol Shields, but a storied woman, the one who makes marks on pages, the woman who claims to answer to the name on the cover of the book, the writer. I do not know the real woman, at least not well enough to count, but I do know this floating and powerful florentine engravement on air who nets fictions as turned and strange as brass rubbings, the articulate spines of fish, slender piles of knuckle bones. The real miracle is that there are miracles. And Carol Shields stories this wonder.

---

1. I have used, taken advantage of, referred to, and quoted from the stories in Carol Shields' collection, *Various Miracles* (Don Mills: Stoddart Publishing Co. Limited, 1985). I trust that the liberties I have taken will be obvious.

(no parrot/no crow/no parrot)

Parrotic lineage: Sheila Watson, Robert Kroetsch,
Michael Ondaatje

Well Kroetsch:
Swore I'd never write another line about you, that bio/critical
introduction to your archival inventory (that you didn't need) like
trying to fuck the wind. Tried but I couldn't come.

Still, the other night I picked up a speedskater in the bar (no
parrot/no crow/no parrot), just a speedskater (second fastest, he
claimed to be) (in which world, I wanted to ask) leaning into the
windless ice. Rapped my unskating ankle propped up on the chair
beside him and told me he was from Philadelphia. Philadelphia –
now do you believe that? – (no parrot/no crow/no parrot) and
asked me if I had a car. Yes, I agreed. I've got a car has crossed the
Battle River and where do you want to go? (no parrot/ no crow/no
parrot). And there I was, waiting for his answer.

Fenceposts, Kroetsch, I want to remind you of fenceposts, just in
case you forget and (no parrot/no crow/no parrot) sitting on any
one of those fenceposts. Bare, under the sky skying itself, hand
between its legs, and you pulling the leaky Battle River behind you
like a boy ahead of a sleigh full of sisters hoping for a long pull. In
a field of snow (no parrot/no crow/no parrot). I am jealous of your
sisters, Kroetsch, every last one of them.

Anyway, this speedskater wanted to drive somewhere, he was sick of skating and so he asked for a ride, and I almost agreed, almost told him I'd show him knob and kettle country, the parkland, almost consented to take him to the edge of the boundary between life and death, to the site of the longest wooden trestle, brag a little, that's what I wanted to do, point out a few contradictions, the lay of the land. Homesick too he made me, with his red ears and his farmboy's hands grappling each other between his knees.

Kissed my first kiss beside the Battle River. Ran my first race beside the Battle River. Lost too. Both times.

And despite (no parrot/no crow/no parrot), wanted to ask some advice. Should I tell him about the frozen dead with their faces chewed by mice? The way that Dried Meat Lake made us imagine fathoms? And that you had all the advantages, you'd already left before I could get started. The Battle River a grassy slur between valleys and you on the north side, me on the south side, but me norther than your south: that's what the Battle River does in its undulations. Heisler and Edberg: two good places for a dance, and fenceposts, Kroetsch, fenceposts. (no parrot/no crow/no parrot) all that was missing.

I admit, I wanted to marry a boy from Heisler, I wanted to play ball in Heisler, Heisler was seething with sex, it sounded like a pair of stockings coming off. (no parrot/no crow/no parrot) around to correct me on that one. Draw me a map, Kroetsch, I did it all wrong.

So I plan to do it right with this speedskater, never confess to ulterior motives, just load him up and start driving, pretend I don't know where I'm going, pretend I haven't heard of words (no parrot/no crow/no parrot). Just as long, he says, as I let him take his skates, those long-bladed tumbrels, he'll be fine, he'll find a surface, glass or otherwise, to glide over. And I'm anxious to see the muscles of his buttocks, his ass, pardon me, his calves, his

ankles. Yes, I want to see him skate the Battle River. I don't care if
it's August, he's so fast he probably can. I expect nothing less.

Parrot and crow, I need you now. How do you drive a
speedskater to speed? How do you drive home? Where do you
find velocity? How do you get your hands on haste? You think
these are easy questions, full of clichés, like a bat out of hell and
all that lickety-split. Don't get me wrong. That was what I had in
mind, lickety-split. But let's get serious (no parrot/no crow/no
parrot). When you're moving that fast, there's no time to wait for
advice. And I'm asking you, Kroetsch, for advice: expostulate,
admonish. *Verbum sapienti* .

I've always got my ass in a sling. Advocation I don't need, and
it's too late for letters of recommendation, but I'd appreciate some
serious advice. Nothing paternal (no parrot/no crow/no parrot).
I've got quite a few fathers and their sons around – but *avise* – a
suggestion for sight. In: cite. We can forget about forethought and
prudence – remember, this guy is a speedskater and while he looks
pretty patient, he's waiting to blade away. You could say I'm
nervous. Advigilance I need, that's it. Fenceposts, Kroetsch,
fenceposts (no parrot/no crow/no parrot). In site. I'm looking for a
haystack to bed down in, one of those famous haystacks around
Rosebush or Dead Man's Hill.

It's all the fault of the Battle River, sneaking around Alberta,
making assignations with creeks and valleys. A misfit river, groping
through the parkland with a quiet ableptical convolvement,
flexuosity devouring its own rivulation. And fish, Kroetsch, did you
fish (no parrot/no crow/no parrot)? Suckers and mud-heads, thick-
mouthed and spiney but alive in that green water, nibbling the
grassy banks that rolled up to the knees. The Battle, Kroetsch, the
Battle. There wasn't anything else, no summerfallow or hiproofed
barns, no chokecherries with their dark sting. The Battle (no
parrot/no crow/no parrot) was all and enough on its own.

Well, you could say that it taught me to drive, me steering this speedskater toward the only arena I know, the valley a bevelled jackpine stadium perfect to observe his race. And this rink – no, this tortuous course inviting collision, those sweet collisions of thighs. Do speedskaters ever fall? Their runners turn in? Bad ankles, Kroetsch, Hans Brinker be damned, I can't skate, all the fault of the Battle River, its knobbled ice, its jerky freezing. I cross it with my car, bridges that I long to blow up behind me, those solid, trusty, green-painted Alberta Highways bridges (no parrot/no crow/no parrot).

The Battle, I want to river the Battle, you already caught all the fish but the Battle is still sucking against its banks while I sit staring (no parrot/no crow/no parrot) into scrimmage, a hand-to-hand job, speedskaters slippery with fast. Everything's been dumped upside-down, all the alphabets scrambled together in the weedy muck of this river, which is why I live beside the Bow now, with its clear gravel bottom, its elegant (no parrot/no crow/no parrot) trout, snobbish and quick. But my alpha rhythms set themselves against the Battle's dilution and shrinkage – it undulates itself all the way down here, two hundred kilometres south – and I can feel the Battle swelling, calling all speedskaters, all of summer's touchment into its solemn cleft.

And yes, it was solemnity I felt poised on the brow of that river's bank, before the car began its downward swoop, before the brown singlet of water under the bridge and the steady acrostics of oxbows looping themselves into the east. Going east the Battle was, did and still is (no parrot/no crow/no parrot) and no apologies for that, expecting itself to be crossed and to be held accountable. To rive, to cleave asunder, from one life to the next.

Crossing the Battle, Kroetsch, was a major move, a split from the world, the home quarter, the musty farmhouse, the slanted ceiling of my bedroom, thirteen yearling yearnings finally daring to imagine themselves, crossing that damn Battle into a new map, fresh with folds.

I want the speedskater to skate along the bank, its sharp drop above the swooped valley, I want the speedskater to mark his fluvial current against this channeled contention: the Battle River, Kroetsch, remember? The trails for cattle, for hikes, for serious parking, knock-up lookout the buffalo jump of pregnancy – didja or didn'tja do it, Kroetsch? The stationmaster had a parrot, and a monkey too (named Emily Carr?) I think, and he used to fall under the train, vertigo, fall onto the tracks, and the train coming out of the Battle River valley after its run through the heavily snowed conifers, its secret stop at Duhamel, puffing in the winter dark at the switch. Waiting for another train to pass, waiting for the Battle to catch up just north of Edberg. Yes (no parrot/no crow/no parrot).

It was the Battle River valley, Kroetsch, I don't know where you entered it or crossed it, but it was all in that valley, there's nothing we can say that doesn't gutter to life from there (no parrot/no crow/no parrot) – yes, the stumble of a candle. Even though you were on the north side and I wasn't born yet on the south side, although you were farther south than I was north, and none of us existed then, no words, no reckless alphabet of craving, no speedskaters.

Recklessness, Kroetsch, the Battle taught me to be reckless, to jump on a runnered sleigh and let go, heedless down that incline of danger, of precipitous slope. The truth is, Kroetsch, I've been given advice (no parrot/no crow/no parrot), told to control my* recklessness, my heedless failings. Advice, Kroetsch, is easy. Recklessness, that pitch, requires embracement, a dedication to falling, the chill exhilaration of the cliff's edge, the river's edge, the Battle River, Kroetsch, the boundary between the Cree and the Blackfoot, the cited site of battles, a reckless riding into the blades of speedskaters. Crimed in steep. Let me remind you, Kroetsch, you pushed Julie off the cliff (*Alibi* 228) of the Battle River valley. Cliff/boom/wreck, the car leaping forward into Battle. And Jeremy too. "They do not even scream as they fall" (Gone *Indian* 158). Recklessness, Kroetsch, you taught us all recklessness (no parrot/no crow/no parrot). Advised us to fall.

So I'm not laying blame – just a speedskater, one lousy speedskater far from home and lonesome, my lust is kind – a table is not a chair, Kroetsch, and you may wield a mean dishtowel, but (no parrot/no crow/no parrot) don't forget fenceposts, Kroetsch, cart-trails, Ferry Point and Meeting Creek where the man that I didn't quite marry came from. Enough to make a woman cry. The Battle River slurring the words between death and dreaming, always there when I thought I had managed to lose it, cross it, leave it behind. And yes (no parrot/no crow/no parrot), when I emerge from the nightmare where I am poised on the edge of the bank ready to fall, when I stick my head above my dream, I always know, in that murderous moment between wakings, that it was the Battle River that heired us recklessness. And my best friend did marry a man from Heisler, let him take her to knock-up point, unhook her bra and get his hand inside her pants, let him try to hold himself back; she had a bang-up wedding, and a big dance, and now she's got three dandelion-headed daughters. You see what I missed? Damn it all anyway (no parrot/no crow/no parrot), I should have been smarter.

Not enough practice, that's what it was, and now I have to get even with myself, retrace my steps and try to make up for the past, speedskater or no, I need a trip back to the lip of that valley, to the selvage of my early world, the membrane between outside and in, and all the things I dreamed of doing, if I could get across the Battle. Reckless, you see.

So (no parrot/no crow/no parrot), I've been trying to take my own advice, parrot and crow myself into position with a speedskater, it's the speed I'm after, and let me tell you, Kroetsch, that is no joke. I want to "bolt noisily and violently out of the present" (*The Double Hook* 85). Whether or not I want to bolt past the past is another question, running backwards takes practice, especially over water, let me tell you, and the Battle River is full of water, Kroetsch, whether or not a person drinks it. And I suspect, after the folds of the hills, the muscles that join the speedskater's thighs to his ass, there is a settlement beside the Battle, a ghostly settlement in the valley, a town full of advice.

> In the town below
> Lived Paddy, the bartender,
> and Paddy's parrot.
> (*The Double Hook* 86)

The parrot, Kroetsch, the parrot is to blame for the riverbank and the bridge. "Over the low railing he could look down to the flowing eddies of grey water" (*The Double Hook* 86). It could have been the Battle, Kroetsch; it was the Battle. And by the time you withdraw all your money and buy yourself a billfold, and by the time you confess that your mother is dead, "How long. . . do you think a body would keep in this heat?" (*The Double Hook* 92), the parrot's advice seems repetitious, a command, and me and my speedskater sitting there, waiting for ice to form on the Battle River.

> It was the parrot who noticed James and Traff first.
> It raised a foot.
> Drinks all round, it said, falling from Paddy's shoulder to the counter and sidling along.
> Paddy looked up.
> James Potter, he said. What's brought you to town?
> The parrot swung itself below the inside edge of the counter and came up with a tin mug in one claw.
> Drinks on you, it said.
> (*The Double Hook* 94)

This parrot, Kroetsch, is a tyrant. This parrot, Kroetsch, extracts confessions from the dumb, me and my speedskater waiting for a little cold weather, waiting for advice, waiting to go backwards over the Battle River and safely into the County of Camrose.

James looked up. The parrot seemed to be watching
him over the rim of its mug.
She was old, James said, speaking to the parrot. It was
the heat that took her and climbing round in the creek
bottom.

(*The Double Hook* 95)

Advising itself into infinite drinks there on the edge of the river,
below the cut of bank, below the car's swoop before we fall, me
and my speedskater strapped into its deep bucket seats, trying to
find a bar without a parrot or a crow, just a little piece and quiet,
just a few draught and tomato juice before freeze-up, to loosen the
thigh muscles a little. And like James, the leftovers embarrass me,
I'd like to get rid of them all, start with a clean bill.

Buy the parrot some beer, he said. It's little enough
he must have to live for. One parrot in this whole bloody
universe of men.
He doesn't seem to care, Paddy said, picking up the
dimes.He gets his way because he's a unique. Men don't
often have their own way. It's not many have the rights
of a dumb beast and a speaking man at the same time.

(*The Double Hook* 97)

Just remember that, Kroetsch, men don't often have their own way,
parrot or crow be damned, it's the silence that deafens us all, the
silence of the fall, the silence of the silent water, in spite of "the
parrot's voice raised on a note of authority" (*The Double Hook*
97), we are the falling and the damned who cannot free ourselves
from freedom even though we try, even though on the edge of the
bank, before we cross the river again, we can see "the lights of the
hotel where the parrot who lived between two worlds was
probably asleep now, stupid with beer and age" (*The Double Hook*
103). Not quite safe enough, Kroetsch, standing in the darkness

above the river, don't forget fenceposts, the reckless recklessness of the advice we take and give (no parrot/no crow/no parrot). Draw me a river, Kroetsch, I did it all wrong. Drinks all round.

You can try to deny it, Kroetsch, you can play poker with my speedskater and tell him you're a grandfather – and he's been taught to be respectful, boys from Philadelphia are, you know, even if they are fast – but you turned that parrot into crow, you were merciless, letting him gloat, letting him give everybody bad advice, insult the world and its readers, sitting there with his black head cocked, never bothering to say *caw*, that black crow you decided belonged with the Battle River, whatever you called that river, all the nameless rivers that we've crossed pouring into the Battle, and (no parrot/no crow/no parrot) what can a poor mangler of alphabets say to this kind of outburst?

> "Liebhaber, you don't know your ass from your elbow.
> You are a *dumbkopf* beyond my worst expectations.
> Don't you see what our friend is doing?. . . Why. . .
> don't you go out to one of Vera's bee yards, take off
> your right boot, hook your dirty big toe onto the
> trigger of a borrowed shotgun, and hope for the best?"
> (*What the Crow Said* 64-5)

You'll shock my speedskater, and I'm trying to get him into position, don't want him to hear (no parrot/no crow/no parrot) the crow calling the parrot black: dummy and asshole, asshole, asshole, total asshole. Let's face it, I'm protective of my speedskater, I want to keep him clean and innocent. I know that "tomorrow 'will be just as miserable as today'" (*What the Crow Said* 82), but I want to pretend different, I want the world to be a road leading to the Battle River, and you're goddamned right we're all scared shitless, what the hell else is there to be but scared, when the only thing we can do is cross the Battle River and spend the rest of our lives taking speedskaters back to that crossing, that

watery gesture across the parkland, parrot and crow citing our
terror, naming our deaths. Fenceposts, Kroetsch, let me remind you
of the gentleness of fenceposts, fenceposts trundling down the
valley to meet the Battle River.

(no parrot/no crow/no parrot). How can I resist? "'*Schwarzkopf
*'" (*What the Crow Said* 97), let me call you *schwarzkopf*, I said to
the speedskater who said, "huh?" he said, reaching under my shirt
with his Philadelphia hands, his hands so long and knobbly in
their touching that I turned into a river right there.

Make me an aqueduct, a conduit for the Battle River crying
itself across the goddamn country, the high cry of a perfect falling
into grace (no parrot/no crow/no parrot), there is still a bridge and
there might be a river, even a speedskater, a daredevil who builds
air and who climbs sky and time, "mercury slipping across a map"
(*In the Skin of a Lion* 35), Michael Ondaatje's parrot naming the
future, silent and adviceless to the fallen.

> A South River parrot hung in its cage by the doorway
> of the Ohrida Lake Restaurant, too curious and
> interested in the events of the night to allow itself to
> be blanketed. It watched the woman who stood dead
> centre in the room in darkness. The man turned on
> one light behind the counter. Nicholas Temelcoff
> came over to the bird for a moment's visit after
> getting the drinks. "Well, Alicia, my heart, how are
> you?" And walked away not waiting for the bird's
> reply, the fingers of his left hand delicately holding
> the glasses, his arm cradling the bottle.
> (*In the Skin of a Lion* 35-6)

The moat around her, Alicia, and the parrot finally named (no
parrot/no crow/no parrot), its silent advice taken by the woman
who takes its name before hacking off her habit and walking out
into the street. Yes, Kroetsch, the crow was a woman, don't forget

the Battle River and the parrot watching us all leave.

> The parrot Alicia regards her departure and then
> turns its attention back to the man asleep in the chair,
> one arm on the table, palm facing up as if awaiting
> donations, his head against the wall beside a crest.
> (*In the Skin of a Lion* 41)

We leave, we never leave, we return endlessly, even without the excuse of speedskaters or advice, even old and knowing better (no parrot/no crow/no parrot), reckless, Kroetsch, reckless.

> Now the parrot has a language.
> (*In the Skin of a Lion* 37)

Drinks all round.

In Australia, Kroetsch, I saw parrots, I flew with them. Flapping the sky white in Canberra, the green morning drawing them out of the trees and into flight. And above the graves at Kalgoorlie and Alice Springs, turquoise commas swooping their hoarse advice down to me. Kroetsch, fenceposts are useless in Australia. There were no speedskaters to take back to the Battle River and the rivers, Kroetsch, were dusty beds with measuring sticks beside them. Still (no parrot/no crow/no parrot), there were parrots, and maybe crows squawking advice. I heard you.

> *The water flows both ways.*
> (*The Diviners* 370)

And Kroetsch, you are the Battle River.

Much Love,
Aritha
(no parrot/no crow/no parrot)

An Armchair (Reader's) Companion to Club Cars and Ladies Crossing Canada by Train or Will the Real Picara Please Leave Town (Please Haul Ass):

Reading Paulette Jiles' Manual of Etiquette[1]

Etiquette, she says, etiquette. Ticket. (Ticket to ride. That's the ticket.) A soldier's billet (ha, and that you are lady), a label, a book of ceremonies hidden in a king (*sic*)/queen's palace (*sic*)/purse: a prescribed ceremonial, the formalities required by usage (*sic*) (you got that right), the order of procedure (on top, please), the conventional rules of personal behaviour observed in the intercourse of polite society (more than a mouthful, dear reader), the unwritten code of honour by which members of certain professions (*sic, sic, sic*) are prohibited from doing certain things deemed likely to injure the interests of their brethern (and *sic* again). Polestar Press, this is a pole cat, make no mistake, and all these protestations about etiquette (how lovely French makes the word seem) are mere window-dressing, dear reader, mere manual dexterity, a little wrist action to go along with the rhythm of the train and how do you intend to deal with that, you searchers after correct behaviour and the customs of the court be damned. You are on the train now, and that sweet diagram of the club car is just a distraction, intended to tell you not just where you are but where you might be by page sixty-two (go ahead, check it out).

And don't forget that that nice little train imprint following each title is a fucking locomotive and just in case you don't know what they do, baby, they move on their own power, they are the movers and shakers, empowered, capable of running away. So there. Motion. And this manual might serve as a series of stills from a never untracked camera, a treatment for that film you always meant to get funding for, one scene after another like cars following their locomotion device, although don't forget locomotor ataxia: the spine and syphilis strike again.

So by the time you bend the spine at the opening scene, by the time you get to her (Our Heroine), you should be ready, that is if you've been watching, if you're aware. "She is entraining. . ." (5). Aboard, bored, dragging her life and all those old movies after her, although "the concrete apron" (5) is nice (someone will do a thesis on domestic imagery soon), and the "very swank and pre-bomb" (5) is the least you expect. And that trench coat (your mouth moistens, I know, dear reader) is a sure sign of violence and repentence to come, so who's apologizing, you know she's a tramp and you like her that way, it's her best characteristic; enough of the other kind, this one's got a tin halo, or better yet a plastic one with all that credit card abuse, she deserves to get it, and no, she doesn't deserve to have anyone help her with her bags up the incline of those steep and lonely steps, their metal teeth a thigh stretcher especially for ladies in snug skirts, the kind she is bound to be wearing, a tramp like her. And not only is she a tramp wearing a tight skirt and a trench coat and a hat with feathers, but at last, the truth: she's an American, Our Heroine.

Foreigner be damned, that's a politeness, and in this province, Ma'am, we'll pay you to keep your shoes on your feet and your knickers quietly in place; B.C., lady, is a province, all right, in the truest sense of the word, and don't you know enough not to get caught here? Lady, you ran to the wrong place, you'll be eating out of dumpsters, so get out of town fast, get on the train while you can, bribe the porter if you have to, it's worth it just to escape. And Montreal might be your destination, but anything beyond the border is a bonus, believe me, mink coat or not, you'll have more than enough to answer for if you stay in B.C., picaras aren't allowed, they probably ask for abortions or birth control or both. Hah. Keep your spare heart in reserve and run, baby, run.

She is not thinking about what she should be thinking about, but she's allowed some respite, ladies in distress get a few minutes off to fix their makeup and she's got to worry about that hat, the veil tickling her nose, the mesh giving her dots in front of her eyes. Our Heroine, dear reader, is an escapee and you have to give her a moment to adjust her lashes, movies or not, the old powderpuff has to come out of the bag, you can't have her looking like a tramp, she just has to *be* one. And all the disappearing women that she is anxious to emulate got away with that breathless pause before the whole construction starts to move, locomote, events on film have a past and so does she, whether or not she is wearing an unpaid-for mink coat, or a trenchcoat, or nothing more than a pillbox hat and her sleek trampedness, so give her a moment, time for titles before you get to the scenes.

Not to mention the backing (remember the quandry about tax write-offs), American money versus Canadian money, but it's all the same to VISA funding VIA Rail, the two belong together, cosy, and especially in an action thriller where Our Heroine has to get out of town fast, or she'll be subject to the social service tax, so the truth is, all good movies (and books for that matter, dear reader) are produced on credit, nobody gets paid until after (if only that were true with sex or marriage or both) it's all over.

The VIA Rail train is supposed to look like a snake, and already you know that Our Heroine is a tramp if she thinks like that, there are little garden snakes hiding inside every pair of stolid grey flannels, and you, dear reader, might well be surprised that she doesn't start with the porter (he wants her instead of her two-dollar bill), but of course, that would be giving too much away, and in the movies you want to keep as much suspense as possible available for as long as possible, so she just looks at her triplicate reflection (does this strike you as symbolic, dear reader, credit card slips are in triplicate, don't forget) and reminds herself of how much she loves her hat. Which doesn't necessarily mean that she is in love with her hat, but could mean that she is in love with herself, which is not a falling so much as a failing – she has to be ready for a little self-abnegation if she's going to survive this particular home movie.

Because, of course, although the trip has started (hasn't it?), the train is shouldering around the deep gorges (note the repeated sexual imagery) of the Fraser Canyon, it won't be long before the chauffeur appears, no wait, there are no Rolls Royces in this movie, nor any Porsches or Mercedes either, so he has to be the porter – maybe the brakeman or the engineer – they're implied anyway, all you need is actualization for Our Heroine to meet her completion, the train probably has to leave the tracks in some untoward manner, perhaps by encountering another train. No, wait again, the train is stopping, and the engineer and brakeman will have to stay in their places because the train has stopped for The Man from China Bar.

Now why, dear reader, China Bar? Not why this Man, but why China Bar, lost and forlorn and almost nonexistent China Bar? And on this potentially sybaritic train, this vertebraed domino of moving parts, a romantic presence? She is definitely doomed, dear reader, you can slide down in your seat and catch a few winks because that same Man, defined as the romantic interest, means trouble, of course, but not trouble so much as complication and not complication so much as complicity, not to mention sex, no you won't mention that, not when Our Heroine has a compartment of her own, and The Man from China Bar is of course mysterious, and of course after her ass; why not, China Bar has got to be a sad and probably unsatisfactory place to let the snake out of the bag (that was unforgiveable, but it is all Our Heroine's fault, what with her looking into mirrors and admiring her hat), and the hero may be a long shot but he has to be after more than one thing or it will be a short movie, a short book, well, it's not only a question of size, dear reader, but technique, and whatever else, you will not forget that wonderful epigrammatic and sleek little diagram of a locomotive tailing every heading, an odd position if you do say so yourself.

Anyway, the hero's on board and, just in case you forget, you can always re-read his entrance by keeping tabs on pages sixteen and seventeen, even though the narrator (intrusive sot, the club car itself perhaps?) keeps instructing you to check the diagram on page three, as if that diagram is going to be any help in a crisis. Besides, things have already started contradicting each other: what is Our Heroine wearing and is the hat a pill box or a cloche, depending on which romance you are entering, dear reader, and don't forget that her destination is supposed to be Montreal, so perhaps she will be wearing a beret by the time she disembarks in Montreal (the mirror has already told a few too many lies). But it's a little too early to be talking about disembarkation. Now, there's a word for the end of the picture, not to mention the end of a picaresque novel of adventure and intrigue. Hah. And no, Our Heroine, the hat never saved anyone. He's got the papers on her (The Man from China Bar, that is), although he's been told she is posing as a railroad detective, an arranger of mysterious stories that unstory themselves as the train proceeds west. Well, you'll see how good his report is, won't you? And who ends up posing as what? And who will pay? The nice thing about it (his report) is that it predicates her carrying everything she owns when she disembarks "somewhere east of February." What economy! What a wonderful moment, all actions and all possessions wrapped up together in a tight camera still already prepared for, probably shot first, so that the rest of the entrainment is only denouement (oh that's what you call it, all that hanky panky, embarrassing the conductor like that, hoping to lose face under cover of darkness and the deep rumble of train on track in the night). You've got to end your parenthesis, reader, Our Heroine gets confused.

And just in case you're concerned about that moment when the romantic presence, or the MAN, or the significant other, or the complicating factor, or whatever else he might be (see page seventeen for a list of possibilities: "lies, prevarications, inventions, illusions, stories, pacifiers" (yes, 17), especially the latter, man as pacifier, something to suck on), it is offered again as an instant replay (usually reserved for the holiness of hockey), and all Our Heroine can do in the face of such definitive action is put on her hat. "And he seems to have seen her, his face shadowed by his hatbrim, a five o'clock shadow, a six o'clock shape" (21). He too, dear reader, has a hat, and you are in a world where hats are much more than they are and when those hats come off, Bogey be damned, you can expect trouble. So of course he is in the compartment next to Our Heroine's, and of course he knows her instantly, and of course he knows her story, although she is making it up as she goes along, which is the difference between men and women, dear reader, and quite a big difference too if you may say so, especially because of what it does to those who can improvise. So much for the movies. Just remember that he recognizes her from the title of her story, and that's a dead giveaway for him, he who is also going to be Sitting in the Club Car Drinking Rum and Karma-Kola. Even though he claims to be from Alberta (you know about those men, dear reader), even though he is wearing a watch – which is poor timing in a movie because the hands are never in the right place, just watch his – what's he doing but brushing himself down like a self-employed dresser, even while he pretends to be innocent and asks her the first of all quintessential questions: "'Who are you?'" (23).

Well, she claims to be a railroad dick, of course, usurping the role along with the snake, and yes, it's true, that claim could turn the whole thing into *"plain icky regular prose fiction* " (25). Like it or not, you're stuck with those parentheses, at least there's a story between the curves, between those sweet enclosing quarters of circles. Put four parentheses together and get one circle, which is how the story should end, like the encompassing gesture of a conductor's baton. But it's not enough for Our Heroine, she's got to have a classy exit too, given the advent of the man from China Bar, otherwise known as the romantic interest, or the presence, or the significant other. You can only speculate on how long it will take them to hit the sack, dear reader, since you know that under his coat is a report, and under hers a whole lot of well-used credit cards. But it doesn't do to speculate too much just yet. You're still in B.C.

And because it is night, you should talk about hiding, the concealment of dark and the possibilities unhidden by dark, when all that cannot be revealed is revealed, especially in stories, and even more especially in detective stories, or stories about people pretending to be someone they are not or stories about movies. Do not omit that possibility. And the dreams that reveal themselves in the night are themselves questions, the long routine of question and answer that all readers play with all critics and all critics play with themselves, and here Our Heroine even reminds you of how little the questions ask and how much the questioning faces conceal. But especially good is the clock that is always an hour ahead, even if Mountain Standard Time is good time and not half as cockeyed as Newfoundland Time, and Our Heroine has still to find the watch on the arm of The Man who got on at China Bar a little ominous. Her nightmares are all in order. And what about his? Rubbering on hers, does he have any of his own, or is he like every other man searching for a woman, needing to obtain his experience at her expense? And she doesn't have much credit left, remember.

And thank god that breakfast takes place in Alberta; it would be too much to bear if you lingered over those crevasses and peaks for long. The Man from China Bar has to recognize himself once he hits Alberta, there is nothing for it but to admit himself and he is, of course, ominous, of course on a mission, of course official, with his shoelaces that "cross each other like two single-minded arguments" (31). You might even be inclined to like him, especially if his falling suitcase had hit him on his head. But if he's the self that hands Our Heroine coffee and waits to escort her to breakfast you have to admit that he is turning into a mover, more quickly than even the story expected, a man like him should be more cautious with a woman like her, she has a history, and he is supposed to know it.

Even if he does try to protect himself by lying, even though he claims to have been "'a sound tekkie on an Australian movie'" (34). (Now just a moment, this is getting out of hand. First you were in a movie, and then you were in a detective novel, and there was a lot of confusion about running away from America and running toward Canada but it seems totally redundant to add an Australian movie; besides, their tax breaks are better and their government support much much better, and they aren't ashamed of their scenery, they don't try to make Sydney look like New York or the outback look like Kansas; they don't belong here, throw them off the train or Paul Hogan will wreck revenge and then where will The Man from China Bar be?) And he may claim to be a sound man (ahem), but listening doesn't get a guy to first base with that kind of woman. She wants to be talked to all right, and listening is only a distraction. All the while those hot credit card receipts are burning holes in her purse, and her ears (remember, they were bleeding) are straining for his confession, which will never come. Although *he* is bound to, sooner or later.

What is his occupation? In the book he has to sit on the train and watch Our Heroine and try to remember that it might not be her he is looking for. He even has to invent himself, which is hard going for someone who is supposed to be an impostor looking for another impostor. And if he's a sound man, why do you spend so much time looking at his hands? Despite the scenery, which is passing just as quickly as the train passes it. The Bow River "a celestial lariat" (40), the shiny spires of Calgary, the imprinting antelopes. You want her to stop looking at the scenery and get down to it. To hell with writing letters and imagining Montreal and lost lovers: Our Heroine is on this train now, and The Man from China Bar is interested all right (remember, he doesn't *want* her to be from Seattle). Why do you have to circulate around the knives of the cook, or the flushing of the toilet, or the past, when you have all potential futures here in the shape of a man going nowhere and a woman going where she pleases. Hurry up, Our Heroine, hurry up. This train trip won't last forever.

As for getting yourself together, who needs it, all that eyeliner is going to come off the first time he really rubs a hand across your face. And of course, every actress in every movie has the makeup moment (you even allowed for it before, remember), but right now you're impatient to be done with the past, with television research (now, that's a sad offshoot of *Casablanca*), with bars after work; you want to get back to the Club Car, you want to play a game of Canasta like the best of all possible rich dames do, and you want to get laid. Hurry up.

But because she seems to have created herself out of credit cards, you have to wait for an accredited moment, you have to give the dick (excuse you) from China Bar a chance to ransack her underwear, determine that, yes, she really is a line-jumper, a draft-dodger, a woman on the lam, with seven credit cards and three different names and a raft of unpaid purchases, not to mention all kinds of intentions it is impossible for him to determine. Well, there you are, dear reader, you knew that he had to find out something to complicate the plot. Now he will have to spar with his conscience or his job, or even with his heart. Good. The plot thickens, and since you've seen him in her compartment once (twice?), you know it is possible to visualize him there, it is possible for him to return, and to return again, ransacking or not, perhaps next time there will not only be a body on the train, but there will be a body in the compartment, which right now is empty for his convenience (not hers, remember she is playing Canasta). And of course, he does (spar with his conscience), much to your satisfaction, since he has to work for his role (Our Heroine was born to hers). He thinks of telling her he will take her away from all this, he thinks of giving up on his vocation, he thinks of altering his history, but while he thinks this and watches Our Heroine playing Canasta, he is really trying to get on with the story, its inevitable conclusion that he is an investigator of fraud and she embodies the embodiment of fraud, Our Heroine does (which is why you are so fond of her), and yes, he is getting fond of her too, after all, she hasn't killed anyone (yet), but he doesn't want to leave his safety behind and being an investigator is so much better than being investigated (as every text knows), so he will watch until he sees a rift in Our Heroine's unbelievably facile surface and then pour something into the crack. Cracking all her enjoyment in being a lady, sitting in a club car on the VIA Rail Transcontinental, drinking and dealing Canasta and being taken seriously as a lady – so much better than a woman (who has to work for a living and who rations her credit cards to herself, cutting them up when they become too obstreperous, when they offer too much possibility for escape).

So he's not surprised by her lies, her truths, her confessions, it's you who are surprised, you thought she could manufacture something more exotic than that feeble story about working for a television station in Seattle and getting fired. It seems thin, coming from her, Our Heroine, from whom you expect big things, like in the movies, at least a little steam coming out from under the train when it stops, she really could have done better than confess her origins to him, and he got a hold of all that information too easily, much too easily, men like him should have to work for it, should run afoul of things, should be seduced out of their dedication to their jobs and their investigations. And of course you know he is supposed to represent the man on the train that you have all encountered, the man on the train who follows you to your berth and pushes you up against the door between the cars, swiftly, roughly, a swarthy hand on the breast, a quick upthrust of groin before you break away with both your dignity and your desire satisfied, that's him all right, she doesn't need a diagram, so why does she spend so much time looking at them? There are no clues in diagrams, only solutions, and escape isn't ready for her yet. Nor she for escape, not until she's had at least one quick (languishing) thrill, otherwise why take the train? And although she claims to be looking for clues (remember her occupation as a railroad dick), she is really looking for confirmation that the train exists, that he exists, that he might knock on her compartment door, not with a styrofoam cup of coffee (see page thirty-two), but with himself, no questions asked.

Sure enough, he arrives with peanuts and a drink, and you are relieved to be relieved of the obligatory love scene. At last they can get down to fucking and then they will be able to resolve themselves in fictional terms and you can see Our Heroine off on another form of transportation. Well, he isn't so bad, at least he has the grace to slow down, and somewhere in Manitoba they succeed in dropping their roles for a few moments, although they keep their defenses on, spare heart or not, you've got to be ready for escape, dear reader. Well, there they are, in "the hot sexual ambushes of the dark" (64) and you can only imagine their fears, although their pleasures are quite palpable. Especially considering this is a book and not a movie, where the lights would definitely be out, and Our

Heroine would be allowed only to whisper, and never to cry out.

And it takes them that long to get to Regina? Hell, something is wrong with this train, it is slowing down astronomically, if it takes them all day and all night to get to Regina, something has happened to the good old Transcontinental, and where will that get you? A slowed-down train means a love affair that runs its course before the end of the journey. The destination has to arrive first, so you can only speculate about whether they reintegrate or not.

And worse, if it is true that he is moving on the margins, you are now in the territory of the mis-laid. He is probably a critic searching for a way to infiltrate Our Heroine's text, certainly her good name (her credit). And he is. He has rules (improbable rules), he is on a search, while she (poor researcher) is only a compiler of the past. Just the facts, ma'am. Not enough, poor Man from China Bar, too much. Skip-tracer. The lesser void of detective fiction, the fiction of detectives, tectonics of human coverage and discoverage, not to be confused with leverage and cleaverage, but still, an odd form for the picaresque to take, always a chaser and a chasee, and already in Winnipeg she wants to ditch him, knows this is a shipboard romance and he might be a skip-tracer. And who does this story really belong to? To her, Our Heroine? To him, The Man from China Bar? To you, you and you, dear readers, sitting in your armchairs drinking rum and – wait, stop that now. You're not on a train, you are in a perfectly respectable state of mind, and you are not to run up a huge Chargex bill and skip the country. If you imagine the story belongs to you, you just might do that.

So that the question of truth is only too tempting: where can you go after the pursued and the pursuer have finally connected? Nowhere but to truth, "an absolute concept thought up after the invention of protracted and deliberate lying, which came shortly after the invention, not of speech, but of grammar" (77).

Absolutely, and no excuse, this is what will be laid on your adventuress by your Pinkerton man: the grammar of purchasing. Because, of course, the truth has no place in a novel, or all the place there is. Which is the moment you should change your font to Helvetica (see page eighty), even if you resist the bold type, even if the impulses of a court reporter are present in all of you, you and you, dear readers, daring to write an armchair companion to a train trip, Our Heroine, and her Man from China Bar daring to engage in combat on a moving transportation. And forward momentum isn't a good enough excuse, when you know that sooner or later the train has to stop and the characters have to get off, have to arrive at a destination.

So he begins to suspect her story and she begins to suspect his and you begin to suspect theirs, not to mention Paulette Jiles, she with that pillbox hat on the back of the book, smiling like a porter just unfolded her bed. "'You've got to stop not believing me'" (82), she says, and she is right, a double negative included, even naked they are beginning to doubt each other, and you are beginning to doubt them, like the porter you think, how long can this go on, they're ready to confront each other, lay down the law, or at least invoke the rules. And they have an audience (you are), don't they? What's the use of waiting for one, you are here, indeed unfolding the plot yourselves, so come on Our Heroine, our Man from China Bar. They have each other too, as audience, the questioning and the listening that follows the questioning, and the lies that succumb to the listening and the inevitable double entendres of two characters trying to catch each other out so that at some point in their journeys they can let each other go. And the imaginary body is still there, waiting to be actualized, waiting to come to life.

Although they are each other's imaginary bodies, each other's actual bodies, each other's. And the more deceptive they become, the more they turn themselves into that *"icky regular prose fiction"* (25) so that we know they are rapidly reaching an impasse and what can they do but invent, frantically. Even change the rules, promise endings, offer conclusions. Confront each other, change positions, if it is her story, then why does he get so embroiled? Once he catches her he should let go, get out of the limelight, stop trying to push the plot around. But it seems he is entangled with the possibility of print, not to mention another round with a seasoned sparrer, picara, the real heroine, the one that every Skip-Tracer wants, secretly or not, the story, the credit, the print, the titles, the rules, even the headings and the small diagram of the racy locomotive, the one that never gets away on the page, but that races you through the extent of the novel, the novel that Our Heroine reads and then throws away since she knows there will be an in-flight magazine on the way to Greenland.

Escape again. Ahh.

---

1. All quotations are from Paulette Jiles, *Sitting in the Club Car Drinking Rum and Karma-Kola: a Manual of Etiquette for Ladies Crossing Canada by Train* (Winlaw, B.C.: Polestar Press, 1986).

Appropriations, The Salvation Army, and a Wager

Nellie McClung, Sinclair Ross, and an Argument with Dennis Cooley

How to re/appropriate the prairie, this prairie with its tinge of west, its male visage? This plundered prairie, compliant archetype for the erotics of male space, a seized place. Wrestled into submission under the heavy hand of the expectant father, his thieving confiscation, the heavy body of the errant lover, pretending to be faithful. Women need be spies here, women need be terrorists. Willing to use the tools at hand.

Back to the beginning. The prairie. Can I suffer its naming to name me, the woman writer in/on/with the prairie? Is the prairie of my articulation, my envisaging vision, the same prairie that writers and historians and regionalists and scholars have offered me? Where am I in that space; where do I read/write prairie, and how? Or is that inarticulated space abducted, usurped into a transmuted endowment? How can prairie be fictioned? I read and read and read, looking for *my* prairie in all the texts I sneak into, their impossible configurations. A quest for fiction, a fictional quest. Outside my window the prairie rolls itself into the armpits of the Rockies, and the sky lowers itself in an effort to overcome its own size. Appropriated. Requisitioned. I've been appropriated by a prairie that suggests itself as its own ephemeral naming, impossible naming, unlikely even. I look for the fiction of prairie and I meet the prairie of fiction: male: W.O. Mitchell, F.P. Grove, Sinclair Ross, Rudy Wiebe, Robert Kroetsch. Their great extortionate hoaxes, seductive and noisome. Impossible to drown out. Adulterating the soft, high cries we fling into the windy wind of that testosterone poisoning, that despoliation offered up as romance, freedom, the frontier. Let us maraud then, offer these pirates some reprisal. Let us speculate.

I was talking to Dennis Cooley (Winnipeg friend, poet, critic, male), and he was extolling, yes, the virtues of Sinclair Ross. I was listening quietly, he had me doubting my own doubts, worried about the nature of dust storms and sexual longing and blizzards and why I never permit them in my novels, never entertain their neat chaos. The two of us were reading two different prairies, and I was secretly trying to stop myself from remembering Nellie McClung. A terrible secret, Mrs. McClung, no one knows where to put *her* on the prairie – so they stick her in the attic with the old trunks, or down in the church basement. She'd probably approve of government liquor stores and higher taxes on pleasure, that untrustworthy commodity, but despite the ribbons and medals on the guys, the male gang (Ross, Grove, Mitchell, Wiebe, Kroetsch), I couldn't quite get her out of my mind, she was snagged there in a corner, and we were having a secret cabal together. I was trying to slide my hand into the reticule she carried her notebook in and she was talking about grand larceny. It didn't make sense. General Booth was her boy, and he didn't have the ribbons and medals that Ross and Grove and the rest of the gang sported. He was *Salvation Army.* And somehow, the prairie doesn't seem to have much to offer a moral man like that, although he is a venerable presence in Canadian literature. Timothy Findley tells us that his visage watched over Marian Engel's house: "There was a portrait of General Booth of the Salvation Army hanging in the front hall. I never knew why. Asking why would have ruined it" (37). Perhaps that is the way General Booth should always be dealt with, an ignored presence not to be ignored. He will come back, oh yes he will. But let me return to Dennis Cooley, my prairie friend (poet, critic, male), my fellow purveyor of Sinclair Ross, Cooley and his own spatial rummage, he likes his Christians muscular and playing the glass bead game, every *Soul Searching* vista misprisioned (26-7). Cooley says, with a frown, and an element of hushed doubt, keeping his beer glass authoritatively in hand, "Do you think Sinclair Ross had ever even *heard* of Nellie McClung?" I had, you see, uttered the name aloud, *Nellie McClung,* said it defiantly and with gusto. Beer courage. *Nellie McClung.* Don't get me wrong, I'm not a prohibitionist, and we've all learned exactly how much good the vote does us. But she hangs there, her name in the prairie dust: *Nellie McClung.*

Cooley snorts and inhales half his beer. "Do you think Sinclair Ross ever even *read* Nellie McClung?" He was so sure that I firmly shut myself up, that's what you do on the prairie when you see a dust storm coming. Hell, he was probably right. Why would Sinclair Ross have read Nellie McClung, why would he be writing in her direction? Just because of the prairie? Not good enough, not good enough.

But maybe that's all the evidence needed, the prairie. And why should we believe that those who write don't read, especially their intertextual partners in prairie crime? Let me be a spy, a spy who plays dirty. I suspect, Dennis Cooley, that Ross *did* read McClung. There, I've said it. Even worse, Dennis Cooley, I suspect that he appropriated her prairie and her ideas and even some of her situations. I must be crazy; I'm going to lose my best (worst) literary drinking buddy. But wait, wait, let me go back to the beginning. The only way to read "prairie" is to unread "prairie" as having external genitals, or to be more precise, inside-out genitals. Have women ever had the time, the breathing space, to experience themselves as prairie? What meaning has the prairie for women? How does a woman write prairie? And what if she writes a prairie that becomes the arrogation of male writing, the prairie of fiction?

Looking for the fiction of prairie. Nellie McClung: Sinclair Ross. Let me begin by reassuring you, Dennis Cooley, they were not lovers. I have no evidence for my speculations on their joining, no access to secret confessions. I am guessing now, out on a limb, taking a risk, sniffing out clues. The only manifestation is time, McClung publishing *The Black Creek Stopping-House* in 1912, while according to *The Oxford Companion to Canadian Literature*, Ross published *The Lamp at Noon* in 1942 (715-16). She was ahead of him by thirty years. Can I wager a reading on chronology? It is all I have, that and the (maled) fiction of prairie.

The Black Creek Stopping-House and Other Stories opens with a dedication made palatable only by time. We can all be suspicious of the zealous tone of the invocation here, McClung at her most missionary (and hers is not a sexual position):

> *To the Pioneer Women of the West, who made life tolerable,*
> *and even comfortable, for the others of us; who fed the*
> *hungry, advised the erring, nursed the sick, cheered the*
> *dying, comforted the sorrowing, and performed the last*
> *sad rites for the dead;*
> *The beloved Pioneer Women, old before their time with*
> *hard work, privations, and doing without things, yet in*
> *whose hearts there was always burning the hope of*
> *better things to come;*
> *The godly Pioneer Women, who kept alive the conscience of*
> *the neighborhood, and preserved for us the best*
> *traditions of the race;*
> *To these noble Women of the early days, some of whom we*
> *see no more, for they have entered into their inheritance,*
> *this book is respectfully dedicated by their humble*
> *admirer,*
>
> *The Author.* (Dedication)

McClung is talking toward the women in Sinclair Ross, although he has coloured them with the brush of despair rather than hope, of loneliness rather than cheer. McClung's image of the Pioneer Women of the West is capitally euphemistic, but she sketches a paradigm that Ross appropriates. Truly they have *"entered into their inheritance,"* and their inheritance is that they are doomed to appear, years later, in the pages of Sinclair Ross as embittered, immobilized, and essentially resigned helpmeets to their husbands. Margaret Laurence attempts to mitigate the lot they have been assigned in Ross by addressing the dilemmas that his women face:

> These women are intensely loyal, and as
> driven by work-compulsion as their men, but they
> still long, hopelessly, for communication and
> tenderness with their husbands – who desperately
> need the same thing but can never permit or accept it
> lest it reflect unmanfully upon themselves.
>   (Introduction 9)

Her comments in the Introduction to the 1968 NCL edition of *The Lamp at Noon* almost mirror the invocation that McClung offers to her admired Pioneer Women, but Laurence broaches them with a different tone, a tone tempered by the presence of Ross himself, the intermediary in the fiction of prairie become prairie fiction.

But, I know, Dennis Cooley, the shared subject of pioneer women is not enough to demonstrate appropriation (I know, I know, I know, I know, tendentious arguments), and I had better have some irrevocable evidence if I want to persuade the fiction of prairie and the critics of the fiction of prairie that Sinclair Ross was out there helping himself to Nellie McClung and her characters and their dilemmas. He probably never even bothered to read her. Right? Right. Just take another swallow of beer, Cooley.

But. But. There are echoes, strange echoes that make me

question the constructed purity of Ross and his prairie women, echoes that insist on a re/reading of McClung, that gesture toward her stories? characters? ideas? in an indubitable fictional requisition. The tissue of tracery, its faint aftertaste. Enough to make the woman reading herself into the fiction of the prairie indulge in a little spy-work, a little suspicious reading. Women reading themselves learn to read skeptically. And that faint emanation, that tracing, grows stronger, a thread, a path, a prairie trail. A thief, a thief, I want to cry, but no one will believe me, especially not Dennis Cooley, whether or not we've been drinking beer. Who would want to steal the benighted (and the scholar/critics insist on assessing as badly written, not to mention proselytizing) stories of Nellie McClung? What would be the point? A reading then, just a reading of prairie women, or the fiction of prairie, whichever you will. "The Painted Door" reads "The Black Creek Stopping-House," Ross reading McClung, and doing a quick little *pied-à-terre* of the fictional fingers. One fiction staggers from the text of another. Through a door, a hidden passageway.

A comparative quickie. The novella, "The Black Creek Stopping-House," and the short story, "The Painted Door," both concern themselves with young couples working to make a future for themselves on the prairie. In both fictions the husband is steady and devoted, hard-working to a fault. In both, the husband does not understand the wife's needs and longings. Both wives seem very much unsuited for the harsh life exacted by the prairie (let's face it, they are downright unhappy, irritable – all those syndromes attributed to women when they are in a bad mood), and, more than anything else, wish to be noticed as women. In both fictions another man is conveniently present: dark, sophisticated and seductive, willing and eager to spend time dancing and playing cards. (Card-playing is important to both fictions as an instrument of time and sin and the devil and all that other tempting stuff.) Both women end up alone and terrified in their homes at the onslaught of a raging blizzard (their husbands off dutifully working), and between putting more wood on the stove and peering out of the window into the impenetrable savagery of weather outside (this is prairie literature, remember), both women are completely unnerved, so that when the willing and don't forget able "other man" appears (as if by gothic decree, *deus ex snowstorm*), their overwhelming fear of the elements overrides their usual monogamous wifely care, and they succumb to the gamble of flirtation with the "other man" (the dark, seductive one, the one who has time to shave, the one who knows how to dance). Both women are "caught in the act" by their husbands, who manfully struggle home through the storm because they know their wives will be afraid of being alone. The resultant "crisis" becomes a potent metaphor for prairie as arbitrary and punishing moralistic force, with its unrelenting expectation of high moral fibre, work, forbearance, and suffering. Not pleasure, Dennis Cooley, not pleasure. Prairie fiction.

But at this crisis the similarity between the two fictions divides. Ross's husband deliberately freezes to death in mute reproach when he discovers his wife in bed with the charming bachelor neighbour, but McClung's husband arrives early enough to interrupt the adultery, and the potential seduction is not truncated but continued, is delayed and delayed (always still possible) in a marvellous gamble with prairie and fictional time, until a happy consummation is concluded. The manipulation of time in McClung's story subverts the absolutism of the physical setting of prairie, and ultimately forges an idyllic and open ending, pleasured and pleasurable (in a bedroom), as compared to the absolute and puritan closure of freezing to death in the Ross story. In this equation, the physical prairie brings stress to marital relationships, evoking sharply differing desires in men and women. Which invite gambling and its inevitable outcome: gain or loss. Sinclair Ross, I wager, read Nellie McClung. And re-wrote her fictional prairie into prairie fiction. I wager you at least one beer, Dennis Cooley.

McClung would be horrified at my wager, gambling being the work of the devil, but wager it is in both stories, a game of cards that turns the storm at the centre of both tales around. Gaming in "The Black Creek Stopping-House" is both salvation and temptation. John Corbett gives up card-playing in order to win the hand of Maggie Murphy, who becomes the doyenne of the Black Creek Stopping-House. When he marries her, he promises that he will abjure gambling. But the presence of his cardsmanship from the beginning of the story, and the way McClung lingers over his incipient skill suggest that he will have an opportunity to revive his talent before this fiction of the prairie is over. Indeed, McClung offers him a legitimate reason to gamble and to win (there's pleasure for you, Dennis Cooley!) as a time-stopping device in the story. In "The Painted Door," the cards serve in the same way to stall time. Ann's anticipation of the card game parallels her anticipation of her male visitor, a break from loneliness, but the measured tolling that "cards" take in the development of Ross's story suggests the sexual gamble that will destroy the characters when the card game between Ann and Steven is over, when they stop playing cards and play something else. Pleasure (especially sexual pleasure) is linked to cards, but while in Ross it destroys lives, in McClung it redeems them. The "all-nighter" that the characters enjoy in "The Black Creek Stopping-House" is a good deal more gratifying than the "all-nighter" that Ann spends with Steven in "The Painted Door."

Both gamblers, Steven in "The Painted Door" and Rance Belmont in "The Black Creek Stopping-House," are flatterers, over-familiar seducers, with a devilishly predictable capacity for taking advantage of weather-bound women. And they are beautifully available hands when the women decide to take advantage of a little bad weather and gamble themselves, win some sexual pleasure for a change (from faithfulness). They are the perfect objects of desire, unjudgmental, irresponsible. For Steven, "There had been no passion, no guilt; therefore there could be no responsibility" (117). The same is true of Rance Belmont, who does not care about the opinion of the neighbours, and who is eager to insinuate that he has enjoyed the favours of Evelyn Brydon, without taking responsibility for the consequences (76-7). These men (outsiders, wild cards, unattached, experienced) act as catalysts for the fiction of prairie to expend its passion – in Ross's story resulting in the closure of death, in McClung's story resulting in the happy but open-bedded (yes, open-ended) resolution. Look who's the moralist now. Dennis Cooley, believe me, Sinclair Ross read Nellie McClung, even if he pretended not to.

More obvious than any other appropriation is the overwhelming presence of the prairie blizzard, the blizzard which initiates the opportunity for the sexual and social gambles taken in both stories. The storm opens both female characters to potential seduction, to their own sense of themselves as seductive. In "The Black Creek Stopping-House" Evelyn is figuratively shadowed by her own vulnerability, her reading of the sub-text of the elements:

> All day she tried to busy herself about the
> house, but she worked to no purpose, taking up things
> and laying them down again, forgetting what she was
> going to do with them; strange whispering voices
> seemed to sound in the room behind her, trying to tell
> her something – to warn her – and it was in vain that
> she tried to shake off their influence. Once or twice
> she caught a glimpse of a black shadow over her
> shoulder, just a reflecting vanishing glimpse, and
> when she turned hastily round there was nothing
> there, but the voices, mocking and gibbering, were
> louder than ever. (62-3)

So too is Ann in "The Painted Door" shadowed by her potential seduction.

> She pushed a mat up to the outside door, and went
> back to the window to pat down the woollen shirt
> that was wadded along the sill. Then she paced a few
> times round the room, then poked the fire and rattled
> the stove lids, then paced again. The fire crackled,
> the clock ticked. The silence now seemed more
> intense than ever, seemed to have reached a pitch
> where it faintly moaned. She began to pace on tiptoe,
> listening, her shoulders drawn together, not realising
> for a while that it was the wind she heard, thin-
> strained and whimpering through the eaves. (105)

Yes, Dennis Cooley, Sinclair Ross had heard of Nellie McClung and he'd goddamn well read her too and thought he could improve on her. Read those two passages, carefully, if you can through all the distortions of literary history and its external genitals.

And are these women already seduced, not only by the weather and their subsequent fear, but by the speaking silence that surrounds them, the gaps that have contained them, which they now seek to grasp, re-appropriate, take back? Evelyn hears voices, "trying to tell her something," which are not there, but present, an unspoken speaking. McClung makes Evelyn a hearing listener, an agent of her own eventual sounding. Ross makes Ann a waiting and listening body, an unhearing listener. And a facile reading would make it seem that both women are primed by fear and loneliness for that moment when their respective seducers arrive, passive vessels ready to be seduced by an/other's seduction.

When Evelyn Brydon opens her door to Rance Belmont, she is presumably plagued by fear.

> She seized him by the arm, holding to him as
> a child fear-smitten in the night will hold fast to the
> one who comes in answer to his cries. . . . He soothed
> her fears courteously, gently; he built up the fire; he
> made her a cup of tea; there was that strange and
> subtle influence in all that he said and did that made
> her forget everything that was unpleasant and be
> happy in his presence. (66)

When Ann opens her door to Steven, her gestures are similar:

> . . . at the assurance of his touch and voice the fear
> that had been gripping her gave way to an hysteria of
> relief. Scarcely aware of herself she seized his arm
> and sobbed against it. He remained still a moment
> unyielding, then slipped his other arm around her
> shoulder. It was comforting and she relaxed against
> it, hushed by a sudden sense of lull and safety. (109)

But, but, but. It's perfectly clear by now, Cooley, that Ross wasn't just taking a finger but a whole arm from McClung, and he doesn't stop with the taking. He wilfully appropriates and then re-assigns the agency of the moment. In both stories the women are seduced by the inexplicably human sorrow of the weather, its speaking silence that is a replication for the silence and otherment that they themselves occupy. They are, by the time the men arrive, ready to seize the moment, ready to gamble, to take on the other. They have seduced themselves, and become, through their actively written fear, agents themselves. What is interesting is that McClung writes motherly behaviour for Rance Belmont; he builds up the fire and makes a cup of tea, he is courteous and gentle, worthy object of Evelyn's attention, hardly the tough prairie seducer that you, Cooley, prefer. Both McClung and her character, Evelyn, other him, and best of all, he enters his own otherment with pleasure and facility. But Ross makes his male seducer "unyielding" (yes, he thinks he is improving on McClung, all right): and the woman yields not to him but to his otherness, the moment of release that is imposed on the text with his presence. And isn't it interesting, Cooley, that "hysteria" (109) is literally inscribed in the male text, Ann's womb already a wayward signifier, and all her agency usurped by the *deus ex blizzard* of that male/practice?

So what the hell is going on here, Cooley, besides what is now obvious, Ross out and out ripping off McClung, re-inscribing her situation through his own particularly censorious moralism? These fictions offer paradigms for moments of seduction, prairie reading the woman reading the prairie, slippage permitted, indeed encouraged by the outrage of weather. But what is the equation? Prairie plus woman equals infidelity? That's what Ross and his sycophants (try *Why Shoot the Teacher,* Cooley) have offered, plus a lot of implicit moralizing on the dangerous agency of women. Fiction plus prairie plus woman equals – ? And what about fiction plus prairie plus woman plus blizzard, this *blizzard ex deus* that appears so conveniently? From a semiotic point of view, the blizzard is not a blizzard, but a word screen, a veil veiling the erased presence (read gap, absence, slippage, Cooley) of the prairie, which offers an opportunity, yes, an opportunity Sinclair Ross didn't take, to hear the other voice, that of women, a voice effaced, silenced, and yet, give it a blizzard and it just might erupt, gamble with itself, hear itself think. McClung suspects that and permits both her characters and her readers to suspect that. Ross suspects that, and instantly goes for the kill, Cooley, and he isn't just killing off a character (the husband), committing a little character assassination (the wife), or slaking the rakish suitor's desire. No, Cooley, he is killing McClung, and what's worse, he thinks he has every right to. Ross and his cohorts contend that McClung is a reformer, that she erases the text of prairie with her romance. But her fictioned prairie dares to play, while Ross refuses to gamble. And let's get back to pleasure here, Cooley. Both writers (puritans that they are, Cooley, puritans that they are; you don't enjoy reading McClung because she won't write anyone drinking beer, at least not without losing their agency, hah!) seduce the erotic/the sexual *out* of the seduction scene. McClung daring to perpetrate foreplay gently, courteously, as a cup of tea (now that's nerve, Cooley, nerve), while Ross uses the veil of the blizzard to efface the erotic in the stalwart arm around the shoulder, its comforting lull and safety, and don't tell me that anyone gets any orgasms out of *that* except maybe the blizzard or the card-players, yes, they're the ones having all the fun. In McClung. Do you get it yet, Cooley? Problematized pleasure in every way, but in the end, the gamblers and the tea-drinkers get it all.

One last appropriation. Who painted the door? Where does the painted door come in? Paint, its white melodramatic signage on the hand of Ross's betrayed and frozen husband – the forever stiffened one (118). Ah, what an appropriation, Cooley, Sinclair Ross an absolute thief. McClung's "The Black Creek Stopping-House" ends with an enunciation: a "small white box. . . addressed in a bold, masculine hand" (108) that contains "two squares of wedding cake!" (109). It dashes and raises hope: the feminine/masculine hand opening into that ambiguous white signage.

Marriage or death – which one is the prairie infidelity?

And you, Dennis Cooley, you claim this is all coincidence, the common accident of language and its fiction? All that card-playing, those comforting men, those identical descriptions of the weather, those frosted panes (pains) concealing what is both inside and out, those longing to be seduced but not seduced women who instead appropriate the agency of their own desire, who become *deus ex blizzard* in order to gamble? Wagers be their own dangerous seducers, Dennis Cooley, as is the speaking voice in the silence, the reading prairie.

But have another beer, Cooley. You're probably right that Ross never read McClung. Hell, I can't prove it. But Salvation Army, WCTU, and the weather be damned, McClung re-appropriates the prairie from guilt and repression, infidelity and death, permits her women to gamble, to appropriate agency. Buy me a beer, Cooley. You owe me one, and McClung too, if she'll drink it. Pleasure and thievery: just try and appropriate that.

Ghost Narratives: a Haunting:

of Bronwen Wallace

People You'd Trust Your Life To :

People you'd trust your life to:
people you'd trust your life (story) to:
people you'd trust your story to:
people you'd story your life to:
stories you'd trust your people to:
people/life/story:
trust:
the stubborn particulars of trust:
and story:

There is a ghost in Wallace's stories: moving the words around when she isn't writing: when the story isn't telling: when you (reader) aren't reading. And even when you (reader) are watching, watching hard: concentrating: this ghost wafts past a line: a paragraph: and vanishes into the framing margin. There is a faint whiff of citronnella: *the petit mal* hesitation of almost imprintment: a shadow. Something: a shape: a gesture: something there on the peripheral version of the story.

Wallace's fictional ghost is not a presence discussed at length in narrative theory: by narrative theorists. It is too ephemeral to elementize or define: its haunting too elusive to be made part of the peregrinations of Russian formalist theories: or Bakhtinian (dialogical) theories: or New Critical theories: or neo-Aristotelian theories: or psychoanalytic theories: or hermeneutic and phenomenological theories: or structuralist, semiotic, and tropological theories: or reader response theories: or poststructuralist and deconstructionist theories: of narrative that is, narrative and what it is supposed to narrate. For a good time, you (reader) could look at J. Hillis Miller on narrative (66-79): he has it all figured out. Except for ghosts: their indefinable essence.

Wallace's is no literal ghost: no left-over remnant of some character in a rear-ended story: no fictional ghost harassing a fictional character. *People You'd Trust Your Life To* evokes the ghost of story haunting the very story it attends: fiction's inversely ethereal presence: like a shadow's person.

Narrative suffers the affliction of having to bear too many materialist determinations: "in fictions we order or reorder the givens of experience. We give experience a form and a meaning, a linear order with a shapely beginning, middle, end, and central theme" (Miller again, reframing Aristotle, 69). And what, asks Wallace: in her stories: are the "givens" of experience? Are there any? Are they doing what they pretend they're doing: in either life or fiction? And are those givens somehow responsible: for the ghosts of stories haunting stories?

Whose master narrative determined that narrative should be boiled down to plot and character: setting and theme: structure and temporality? How is it possible to plumb the "deep structure" of story without consulting its ghosts? And how to consult its ghosts if they are unacknowledged, if a narrative presumably needs only, as Miller reduces further): protagonist, antagonist, witness (75). Nothing shadowy moving in the wings of the page. Let alone any notion that the story might have a presence beyond itself: elided: extradialectical. The *story* you'd trust your life to is ambivalent: doubly-uncoded: full of loopholes.

But Wallace's fiction refuses to position itself as icon. It refuses the grammar of formatting. It is willfully corrupt: inconsiderate. It haunts itself. Wallace's narrative problem, her question to you (reader) is: *where is the story people can trust their lives to?* Her serious and fictioned question gestures towards the deepest preoccupation of all narrative but that usually attended secretly: as lacuna: as absence. Except here, in *People You'd Trust Your Life To*, where Wallace offers a tentative extension: the hand of a ghost held out to fiction.

Wallace haunts her stories. Her stories haunt her stories. They haunt their haunting of themselves. The economies of fiction on the lam: narrative on the loose. Mobilized: refusing to succumb, refusing to exclude, arguing its own discrepancies. Theories of narratology be damned: every narrative contaminates the presumed master narrative: in *People You'd Trust Your Life To* there is at least space accorded to story's permeation of itself.

Story ungoverned:
Wallace reading between the lines: space and italics: making them speak: tender towards the story. Her poet's gesture of ghost lines: the narrative beneath: acting as its own double: questioning its presumed answers: refusing to be managed. The slipstream story. Lydia, in "Chicken 'N' Ribs" enacting a mirror narrative: language that she cannot quite control or restrain: language that is not language but *"whatever "* (15): insinuating its strangeness into the dominant narrative: surface normality: the ostensibly seamless order of events. Which is only that of a woman eating a meal: with

her three children: in a Swiss Chalet. How pedestrian can a plot pretend to be?

The story's ghost is an insistent undertone that makes itself heard past the background noise in the restaurant: *"And it serves you right, too, fuck-head "* (23). Its dazzling irreverence: *"Christ, there should be laws against this kind of bullshit"* (22): uncontainable inappropriateness: gestures as the ghost of Lydia's story speaking for itself: sliding into the text and announcing itself the way that Lydia would like to: in her imaginary speeches:

> Suddenly, she wants to stand up in front of everyone, tap her coffee cup with her spoon, make an announcement.
>
> *"I'm Lydia Robertson. These are my two eldest children, Richard, who plans to become a mechanical engineer, and Karen, my only daughter, who will study marine biology. Save the whales, maybe, or the whole ocean. I have raised these two, along with their younger brother, Tony, on my own for the past fifteen years, while at the same time finishing my high school education and becoming a nurse. I am now a supervisor of nursing in the OB unit at the General. I want you to know that I have accomplished all this, alone, with minimal help from my family and without any assistance, other than the obvious and easily performed biological one, from my husband, Ken, a no-good bastard who, who. . ."* (30-1)

Her story's spectre goes so far as to almost-intrude on the story: speak past the silencing master narrative of expected behaviour played out in a family restaurant. And the ghost of Lydia's story: with its subtext of Ken's story: his note as inside story: ("Inside the lunchbox was a plastic bag full of marijuana and ten 100 dollar bills."):

Dear Liddie,
Look, I'm sorry, but I can't take anymore of
this. I've got to get out while I can. I hope what's
inside will get you through the worst of it. You can
tell the kids whatever you want. I won't be back.
Don't try to find me. Please.

love, Ken (21):

haunts Lydia. She tells the kids: "'Daddy isn't coming back'" (23):
but at the same time, she *cannot* tell the kids: "whatever she
wants": they keep telling her (now that they are almost grown):
how weird she is: to control herself.

Lydia is excluded from her own story: trapped by her never
having spoken her secret self: by her "one and only life, whizzing
by her as if, after Ken left, it had no time for her" (29). Lydia's
"spiritual experience": her desire to speak past the overt story: is
prompted by her story's ghost: her life's haunting. When she says
Ken's name aloud (31): and begins to articulate her effaced story:
she is freed from the rigidity of her prescribed family narrative: she
is then free to buy every flower in the shop and step into the
"other" wedding story that she witnesses in the restaurant: that she
is so interested in as a shadow story of her own. Lydia: "laughing
and laughing as she enters the small pause where everyone seems
to be waiting for her" (33): is a ghost made flesh: her own story
come to life: escaping the plot she has always been constrained by
and walking through an open door: into a story she can trust her
life to.

Story censored:
But more than unrestrained story, Wallace grapples with forbidden narrative: not only restrained or unrecognized but deliberately suppressed narrative: censored: never legitimized: and yet it too a ghostly presence on the verge of making itself visible. This story that haunts the patriarchal narrative: clots together power, abuse, and sexuality: terrible spirits rebelling more and more against the set and established pattern of narrative.

There are no givens in the chaotic grammar of sex: the very refusal of the male master narrative to give sexual stories substance if their originators are women: these stories approach themselves through an insubstantial moment. Like Mr. Simpson in "Fashion Accents" whose "voice was smooth and patient, like chocolate syrup and him just pouring it on until he'd coated everything" (50): the narrative of sexuality is haunted by its own censorship, the thick sweet chocolate syrup of patriarchal obfuscation. In "Fashion Accents" Wallace incorporates the very problematization of the presence of sexuality by effacing it: wrapping it in nail polish and lipstick: Stella's scarves and heels and indefinable style: again presence of an absence, an unstated narrative:

> Stella's nose was too large, her eyes too close together,
> her mouth was crooked. But she was beautiful, Stella.
> Even then I knew that her beauty had to do with what
> was called style. I also knew that I needed some badly,
> since I was not going to be beautiful in the normal,
> easy way that some of my girlfriends seemed to
> manage. . . . I was awkward and skinny; my hair was
> too straight to be left casually alone. I needed style. At
> the time I thought it was something simple,
> something you could learn by watching. (38-9)

Physical style: like narrative style: intangible: a ghost presence between the lines of actual appearance and illusion. Style is what enacts Hutcheon's incredulity toward metanarrative (1989, 39-44): is, in effect, the element that must negotiate the fixations of narratology.

Stella contaminates Brenda's "givens": those that have been imposed on her by her upbringing: her parents: her limited experience. At exactly the narrative moment that Brenda is poised on the brink between eagerness and fear at her developing sexuality, Stella introduces the possibility of multiple and alternative narratives:

> I was beginning to see that there were a lot of ways of doing things, of living, that I'd never really thought about. My parents made it seem like there was only one way and up until now I had accepted that, at the same time as it made me feel rather, well, *discouraged*. So when I say that Stella suddenly made my life seem possible, what I really mean, I guess, is *possibilities*, ways of getting on that I thought I could manage. (45)

Narrative magic: the story doesn't have to follow the same pattern all the time: there are differences ghosting themselves as possibilities.

Indeed, the very story of the story of the story is ghosted in "Fashion Accents" by Stella's husband, who acts as pimp for the model narratives of movies: the movies that Stella and Brenda go to together: where they are free to react to those implanted/imposed narratives by holding each other and crying for fictional tragedy:

> They seemed so vulnerable, those women on the screen, and so grown-up at the same time, running towards or away from some huge, terrible event. I

suppose it was really myself I was crying for then,
wanting my own life to be as huge and as terrible as
theirs. (49)

Brenda wants her own life-*story* to be as huge and as terrible as the
life-stories of the women on the screen. She does not want the
articulated but diminished life of her mother: who insists that
childbirth is the most quickly forgotten pain in the world but who
is unable to reconcile her officially tempered version with her
"real" memory of the horror of her giving birth to Brenda. And
when Brenda's mother finally succumbs to the story her memory
insists on relating, it is a story that Brenda can only overhear as a
ghost: an unknown presence (just back from the high-pitched
tension of discovering her own sexual narrative): caught on the
landing between floors (or pages).

   In laconic circularity, Brenda's overhearing of this terrible story,
so unlike the model narratives imposed on childbirth and sexuality,
evokes the ghost/memory of the run-away Stella as sexual narrative
in and of herself: present in all sexual references:

But all of a sudden, there she was, inside my head.
Stella. Her smoky, spicy scent was so strong that, for a
moment, I thought she really was there, upstairs, in
our kitchen. I could even see her at the table with my
mother, and me there, too, somehow, sitting between
them, listening. (54)

It is the stubbornness and mystery of these women that moves
Brenda: her hearing the suppressed narrative of childbirth as
climax to sexuality that makes her feel she has made an enormous
discovery. And it is a story that has to remain unacknowledged: a
ghost story: Brenda cannot "let on" (55) that she has heard her
mother's narrative of her own life's beginning inside her mother's

body. Story: within story: within story. Sexual story so suppressed that it is reduced to a narrative of indirect blame: everything blamed on sexuality, but repressed so that in the actual narrative is a gap, an absence. Only when Brenda enters the ghostly narrative of sexual experience herself can she understand her own helplessness in the face of its taboo story.

The ghost story of sexual abuse is even more rigidly censored: haunted by anger: a narrative trapped in its own disbelief. Lee wants to announce: loudly: incontrovertably: her fear of the dentist who abuses his position to fondle her: she wants to denounce him in a daily narrative voice the way her sister feels free to declare her physical need to urinate:

> "*Dr. Allan's been feeling me up, every visit,*
> *for the last three years.*" I imagined saying this, out
> loud, in Lawson's, just after my mother had ordered
> the sundaes. "Feeling me up" was the perfect phrase. I
> imagined saying it in the clear, unembarrassed voice
> with which my sister Jill used to announce her need
> to pee. The voice of someone who doesn't give a sweet
> shit whose [sic] listening, someone who knows her
> rights. (138)

The fact that Lee never tells the story: never dares to tell the story: speaks to the essence of the ghost narrative at work. Her story would be questioned: would not necessarily be believed. She cannot imagine articulating this scenario: and it is then that she knows what terrible danger she and her sister are in. The story that cannot be told is the story that holds us in thrall: that can do with us what it will. Without being able to narrate what is happening: censoring herself as she is censored by her parents, especially her father: she is powerless. Only when she gathers courage to infiltrate the master plan and refuse passivity: by sticking the dentist with one of his own tools: a dental pic: can she enter the narrative. Her action is its own accusation: and she only says: "'You know'" to the dentist when he asks her: "'What in hell do you think you're trying to pull?'" (142). He tries to take narrative control back from her by saying: "'Just remember. No one's going to believe you. . . Who were you going to tell anyway, sweetheart?'" (142): but he never touches her again: which can only mean that he has been forced to recognize her ghost presence in his deliberate strategy. She is no longer helpless.

Still, her story is a ghost story that continues to haunt her with its silence. She wants to tell her mother: her father: her sister: everything, but she never does: and in her reconstruction of the story, she mistrusts her memory: "Perhaps what I don't remember is worse, even, than what I do" (145). More important is Lee's mother's admission of the potential story in the letter she writes to Lee when Dr. Allan dies: "*I can't help thinking of you girls and that drill and no freezing*" (147). Her admission of the possible missing narrative is an offering: an apology for censorship and disbelief to the ghost narrative never permitted. So that the ghost of Lee's untold story is echoed by the ghost of her mother's inexplicit acknowledgement that there might have been an untold story: that danger did lurk in the official version.

ᙅ᎒ ᙅ᎒

Story Intuitive:
"Back Pain" tries to decipher a ghost story in the same way: glancing at that story only as emanation, a "Mothers' Early Warning System" for narrative dysfunction: erasure: not quite present in the text: "Something is wrong. Something is wrong with Kate, but Barbara doesn't know what. Doesn't know what to ask,

that is, or even if. And then what?" (97). How can event be plotted if it is not event? And even if the "something wrong" is admitted, its ghost is not so easily assuaged. Can what is absent here be reduced to plot and character? Whom to trust here: the person? the life? the story? the instinct? Or the ghostly emanation on the periphery of the surface narrative?

> Something is wrong. Something is very wrong
> for her daughter, Kate, and Barbara knows it. Knows
> it, but doesn't believe it.
> No. Scratch that. She believes it all right. She
> just doesn't know what to do about it. (102)

The story is: and then the story is: and then what? Which narrative can be trusted? Barbara's instinctive sense reads between the lines, recognizes the ghosts of fear and anxiety. Whom can you trust? What can you be certain of if your daughter's boyfriend is battering her?

Only the story: Wallace tells us: only the story as it is peopled by the trust of the people you'd trust your life (story) to. "If This is Love" stories exactness as ghostly: open to doubt: "The history that matters is the history we can use" (57). In *Lives of Girls and Women*, Alice Munro encapsulates our attempts to remember precisely, to inscribe our personal narratives: "The hope of accuracy we bring to such tasks is crazy, heart-breaking" (210). Something always slips past us: inexplicable. Even prescriptions cannot save us from the ambush of surprise: the ghost story of "Another country heard from" (62): ghost knowledge drifting into the narrative we have established as believable: the one we, perversely, want to test. How can Allison know what music her mother listened to while she was in the womb? And how can the limits of story: of body: of allergies or death be tested? Allison's allergies are her body's inscription: an inner story, only intuited.

Story Braille:
Memory may be hopeless, but it has the braille of fingers reading re-inscription. In Wallace, there is always the possibility of the doubled narrative: the twice-written story: the re-lived life: re-marriage to a first love ("Heart of my Heart"): the repeated events of marriage, birth, death, part of the master narrative, yes, but also their own shadow stories: idiosyncratic ghost spirits of the past invading the dominant narrative. Like scars rippling the surface of the skin, marring its texturality: the burn marks blooming around the waitress's wrist that Lydia ("Chicken 'N' Ribs") suddenly wants to kiss (25): the scars where Linda ("Heart of My Heart") has tried to cut her wrists, "covered with Band-Aids that had been stuck on any old way, dirty and puckered, so that beneath them I could see the masses of crude, ineffectual cuts and scabs" (9): the scar on the back of Gail's hand ("People You'd Trust Your Life To") where her husband closed the door on her hand the first time she tried to get away (150, 168): the scar where a prisoner ripped Roy ("For Puzzled in Wisconsin") open in one swipe:

> Across his middle, from his belt line to just
> below his left nipple was a wide, jagged, white scar.
> He had a lot of hair, but it hadn't grown back over the
> scar, which was thicker in some places than others. It
> glistened and bulged in the yellow kitchen light,
> stretched taut over his gut as if the skin couldn't
> take much more. (85)

Scars speak their own mystery of what has been done to the whole and perfect skin of narrative: they speak interruption to the body's story, its capacity to accept inscription. For Anna, Roy and his scar are a story that she likes to tell: and she tells it often: although it is only a part of the story of the summer she worked as a waitress at a lodge in Muskoka.

Scars are also faint signposts to narrative and shadow stories of their own: perhaps stories that can only be read with braille: Wallace's special braille of touch:

> what I can see now is a close-up of Joan's hand,
> reaching out to Roy's bare gut, caressing it so
> intimately I can't believe she's doing it in front of us.
> And then, with the tip of her index finger, gently, very
> gently, she traces the scar, every turn and bulge, from
> Roy's nipple to his waist, as if to show us exactly
> what it's like.
>   As if his belly were a map, almost, and the
> scar was this road she was pointing out, wanting us to
> see where he'd been. And where she'd been too. (86-7)

The trust required of touch becomes an emblem of narrative and memory: touch its own ghost whispering past the guidelines of expectation.

Story Presence:
But despite memory, Wallace knows the harbingers of recognition that ghosts bring to the stories they haunt. Presence: photographic presence recognizable. The teller in "The Scuba Diver in Repose" telling finally in her photographs the story of presence and the presence of absence. She claims that being a teller (telling money presumably: in a bank presumably): is her "real" work: that

photography is "'just a hobby'" (174): but she is a teller/ghost for
the photographer of the invisible. Her photographic attempts to
capture presence (past obvious physical presence) as an absence
enable her to evoke previously unknown (unwritten) recognitions.
The teller/narrator/photographer (Gillian Stewart) in this story
tells a narrative of inverse death: the way that story can come to
life and pay attention to itself, as she does (176): in the same way
that it can refuse to recognize itself, as some of her photographic
models do: "one of the women from work, Helen, was actually
angry. My parents didn't even recognize themselves" (178). The
teller has no special access to a bank of information, but forces us
to recognize what we have never seen before: and her story is
haunted by its own haunting. Diane Arbus's line, "'It's what I've
never seen before that I recognize'" (182) becomes the teller/
photographer's reprise: becomes the story's reprise: becomes the
reader's reprise: the choric voice/ghost that points to presence
previously unrecognized. Recognition becomes a haunting. The
teller of the tale can photograph the impossible: the unseen: the
story's ghost:

> I began to see that very often people were most
> themselves when they didn't look it, when they were
> unrecognizable in all the usual ways. (177)

In seeing the document/story/photograph, we too become witness
to the ghost presence: implicated in bank robbery: the teller's
hoarding (a banking impulse) of photographic detail
(representational images): detail that tells all that we do not know
we know but that we recognize. Not plot: not characterization: but
the instant of refusal, the person known as they are not known: as
"other" to their usual story/representation. The obverse narrative:
not simply unexpected but invented. Presence: knowledge that
materializes in a developing tray.

And does the teller not determine how and where the narrative can die? When Jimmie (the scuba diver who dives beneath the surface: who can recognize what he's never seen: who insists on the teller/photographer learning to look: seeing what is not there but nevertheless present) dies, the ghost of his death becomes the presence that the photographer/teller does not want to record or recognize because once she does she will have to efface herself in order never to see it.

Again, the spaces in/between the story provide for the presence that is so absent to the grieving narrator: but those spaces also leave room for the breath of the story's ghost to breathe: along with the breath Gillian has been holding for a long, long time: until: until: until: at last, she can turn the narrative's face to the light: permit its angle of recognition. The beauty of this story resides very much in its hauntedness: the teller/photographer's inability to tell, and yet the inevitable necessity of recognition as telling. And in the end, the destroyed photographs (impossible to replicate in narrative) become the story's ghosts: absent and present: both extant and destroyed.

That "The Scuba Diver in Repose" completely undermines the notions of content and characterization that you (reader) clutch so determinedly is only a small part of the way that the narrative haunts itself. It is even more brilliant for its implicated but subversive employment of death as the traditional narrative ending. Along with the death of narrative's focus on death as a happy (*sic*) ending motive is the (narrativized) death of the character Jimmie: but even more complex and moving, the actual death of Wallace herself (extra-narratively). It is as if she is writing from beyond the margin of death: as if her own dying haunts the presence of absence in these stories she wrote just before she died. At the same time, this presence utterly explodes the narrative convention/element of *denouement*. Truly, the reader/witness is haunted here by haunted story.

 C9 C9 C9 C9 C9 C9 C9 C9 C9 C9 C9 C9 C9 C9 C9 C9 C9 C9 C9 C9 C9

Story De/Railed:
Expectation resists the story that is trying to tell itself, complete
with ghosts. "'That's what I'm tryin' to tell you, goddamnit!'" (149-
50) Gail declares at the beginning of "People You'd Trust Your Life
To" and on the heels of her own declaration wonders about her
son: "'Maybe he's trying to tell me something and I'm too stupid to
get it'" (150). What story is the story trying to tell us? The four
women of Good Girls Gobble and Gossip Group (G5) recount
their stories to one another regularly: they behave reprehensibly:
they talk volubly: they rail at one another. They become masters
(sic) of each other's narratives, but never permit themselves to sink
into a master narrative.
    They worry about their children trying to change their life
stories. They themselves have changed their own stories: Selena's
three and a half incarnations: from Susie Patterson to Suzi to Suzi
Sims to Selena Bluestone: re-writing herself to suit her own ghost
narrative. They have all, the four women, chosen their names and
their colours to camouflage themselves: yet, they count on each
other: they place their living narratives in one another's hands:
they count on each other to read this slippery and deceptive story
called life: to read between the lines.
    Myrna imagines the four women as they might be read by the
people next door: "how they must look. . . .All lit up like this, the
stereo blaring. . . Four middle-aged women sitting around a table
full of dirty dishes in a kitchen that looks like it's been through a
war, getting drunker than hell" (164). They are, these four women,
in their narrative insurrection, going through one another's stories:
infiltrating the narrative: the tension and the setting, the climax and
the *denouement*. They are destined to partake of one another's
plot: to slip a word in here and there. They have engraved their
mutual and distinct histories: they trust each other with their lives

by trusting each other with their stories: the ghost narrations that save them. They traverse the countries of each other's futures: and they know the secrets and the hauntings of their inside lives. These are the people you can trust your life/story to: separate from the master narrative of judgment or expectation: the rigidities of protagonist/antagonist/witness. No divisions here, only the beautiful bones of narratives that have escaped the cages of their prisoners.

These are people you'd story your life to:
Stories you'd trust your people to:
People you'd trust your life (story) to:
And, reader, here it is.
Ah, reader, these are hers:
Bronwen Wallace.

Nude Travelling:

for Henry Kreisel

Henry Kreisel, you put your long and elegant Viennese finger on us, your story reading our reading of our Albertan (read not so provincial as all that) cultural selves, we doubters, that story you wrote, so the story goes, in the hospital for some bodily misbehaviour, in 1959 (inspired by Norman Yates and read aloud to Eli Mandel), measuring so infallibly our fear of art's brave nudity.

The truth is, your story inspires desire. I confess, I want to be the travelling nude. I need a new job anyway, a change of career would do me good, I'm getting stale on my students, boringly repetitious and Mahler, well, I've always associated Mahler the musician with flight, those enormous rhythms sweeping through the Jack Singer Concert Hall, especially the spot in his First Symphony where you can detect the faint strains of *Frere Jacques*. Yes, Mahler your painter's okay, despite his lack of talent, his imitations of other *mahlers*, and although I have a sneaking sympathy for his father (well, would you want a son like that?) and mother (her secret and gentle assurances), I have to come down firmly on Mahler the would-be-painter's side. After all, he envisioned her (with your consent of course), the travelling nude, that is.

119

And not just because I need a job, need to pay the rent, make a version of living. No, it's her (the travelling nude's) responsibility I crave, that moment when she walks into Elks' Halls and school gymnasiums, when the folding metal chairs stop scraping and their eyes rest on her limbinal (not to mention libidinal) arrangement, when she incites their charcoal to stroke the surface of the drawing paper. It is the kind of iconic occupation that we all wish we had, and me especially, I admit it. I want to be able to stop people in their tracks, make them hesitate, pay attention to culture.

Now, don't get me wrong, I am not immodest. I haven't the talent or the practice of Mahler's Valerie. First of all, she's in better shape than I am, I've got a few years on her, although I'm not a complete loss as a figure of speech. My breasts are good, firm and shapely, and my legs still long and tapering enough. I've got a little belly (which is what happens when you sit behind a desk all day, marking student essays, another good reason to change careers now, before it's too late), but that only adds texture, character for the potential strokes of charcoal. And unlike poor Valerie, who has a gap in her smile, my teeth are perfect: a straight line, milk-white, flossed and brushed three times a day. Although the history of my teeth relates to why I am interested in this job, in its opportunities for travel.

I had cavities when I was a child. It's the truth. Well, I didn't get a lot of candy, but my parents were poor – we were poor – and dentists were low on the list of farm family necessities. And when the holes in my back molars finally demanded attention, they took me to the butcher/dentist of Camrose, he who would give butchers (and still does, I suspect) a *good* name. They didn't know he was brutal, a child beater, shook me and slammed me into the chair more than once because I cried tremulous tears at his less-than-gentle knuckles in my then small mouth; they thought I invented my protests because I didn't want to go to the dentist. Dutch Calvinist parents are a suspicious lot: they always believe their children least and last. So my parents resisted taking me to the dentist because it cost so much money, and I resisted going to the dentist because he hit me and yelled at me (probably part of his technique; I heard him on the CBC the other day bragging that all his kids have become Olympic pole-vaulters – imagine the shock of waking up to that voice revisiting my childhood trauma – and I suspect you only become an Olympic athlete if your parents yell at you, although mine yelled at me about *not* reading so many books). When I finally became a university professor and was required to enroll in a well-flossed dental plan, I found a woman dentist who taught me to trust her (women dentists have small hands, none of those male grappling hooks trying to insert themselves into your mouth), gave me headphones to block out the noise of the drill, told me to raise my hand if I felt the slightest twinge of pain, read my books, reassured me about the potential humanity of dentists. The reason I have no unfortunate gap in my front teeth is her patience, and the delicacy of her hands. On that score, I have one over on Valerie, the travelling nude. Although it is clear from your story, Henry Kreisel, that her blemishes enhance her desireability (as a nude, travelling, female, that is).

Oh, the gentleness of your invention, Henry Kreisel, the pure picara of her travelling. I should be covetous of Mahler the painter (his potential fame alongside *Voice of Fire* in the National Gallery) or his famous namesake the musician and his bombastic symphonies. I should be coveting the job of painter or composer, not their peripatetic muse, her rambling evocations. And no, not muse, but model, a more exemplary occupation, a measurement, a standard. But I want the job of travelling muse, I want to wake up lazily in the Calgary sunshine (do you mind if the nude travels out of Calgary instead of Edmonton?) and know that on Monday morning I will get up, shower, dry my hair, put on the slightest smudge of lipstick, sling my purse over my bare arm, slide my feet into my shoes (low heels, Mahler, that's the one aspect of your vision I resist: high heels give me sore feet and a sore back, and I have some right to determine my working conditions), and stroll out the door to the waiting cab (always a Checker, they are the most respectful), which will take me down to the depot, and although I can think of classier ways to travel than the dog, there is something endearing in the way that the drivers always tip their hats to me, the way that the other passengers fall respectfully silent when I trip up the stairs and select my usual seat near the right front of the bus. And whether I am going to Three Bear Hills, or Great Fish Lake, or Pollux, or Castor, or Stettler, or Heisler, or even Camrose (and yes, someday I will walk into my old dentist's office, right into the room where he is scaring the shit out of some newly unfortunate child, and deck him with my purse, which is large and heavy and will have some impact), I am always anticipatory of the way the landscape will unfold past the window beside me, of the way that we will stop for rough coffee at a local gas station, of the cultural potential of Alberta, which I, the travelling nude/muse, am arousing and endorsing with my mere presence.

Henry Kreisel, you knew Alberta (that province of provincialities) well. The travelling nude's job is "to help along the growth of culture in the land" (111). What a challenge, fit only for Alberta, for Alberta Culture funding (Alberta Culture has taken over from the original providers, the Extension Department of the University of Alberta, of short courses for the "rough diamonds" (114) of undiscovered *mahlers*). Of course, Mahler went to a respectable art school, *The Ontario College of Art*, and as his father noted, "'The building is beautiful. Big solid pillars. Good stone. Nice trees all around. . . . Respectable. Quiet. Clean. Not like those attics you hear about. Well, maybe there's something to this art business after all'" (112). Mahler graduated and took his job with Continuing Education long before all this recent business came out about *The Ontario College of Art* hiring women to offset the traditional racism/sexism of the school, an affirmative action programme, which will perhaps ensure that there are as many male models (travelling nude) as women, and that their footwear will be just as uncomfortable. A good thing too; Mahler's father would have been terribly disturbed by the controversy. He knows art is a dirty business, and this public outrage would merely confirm his suspicions about the value of his son's training. Poor Mahler. If only people like his father would understand academic intention, learning for its own sake. Of course, my parents aren't going to be very pleased when they discover that I have given up a perfectly good job in a clean, well-lighted classroom for provincial nudity and travel. They had enough trouble with me over dentists and reading, they were relieved when I finally grew up, became academically respectable or respectable if academic.

And as for the outrage that Mahler aroused with his suggestion, the wives boycotting their husbands' eager support of the travelling nude, it would shock Mahler's parents and mine to know that now the travelling nude is supported by the wives as not wives but artists in their own right; they have voted for the male body as model for the human figure, and their pencils are eagerly poised when he appears to offer them his poses of David or Daniel, of workman or thinker.

Besides, I have a small reputation of my own, as a trouble-maker. Alberta Culture isn't going to enjoy footing the bill for *me* as the travelling nude. I've caused them no end of pain and heartache with my criticisms of their policies and their incentive grants. But Valerie has quit, simply refuses to continue; the cold gives her chilblains, she says. This is the Valerie whose name means truth, who lacks a surname, and yet is not nameless, is forever named as the principle of art in conflict with its own imagination (*Another Country* 148).

Well, I've got both the imagination and the circulation of a caribou, a northern resilience, twenty below or steamy chinooks make no never mind, and the weather conditions of this job suit me just fine. Ah the feel of air, the irresistible un/clothing of skin ("wouldn't it be chilly with no skin on?"), and all it speaks, a pure text without the need for authentication or bibliographical elucidation. It is the call of cutaneous occupation, epidermal, integumental, how pelt conveys itself as speaking subject despite being the gaze object of so many miniature *mahlers,* their greedy glance. Skin as a metaphor for life, survival; and its friction that resistance to air dragging itself over the body's planes. There in the rasp of charcoal on heavy paper, in the old smell of turpentine from last week's oil's class, I will enact my professional expertise, that of a woman with skin, the travelling nude. Not something I want to slough, this outer layer confining my bone and sinew. Roetke's "shapes a bright container can contain." My skill this envelope, this embrace, and yet external to all knowing, all sensation.

So Henry Kreisel, Mahler's vision of Valerie makes "The Travelling Nude" and we reading you read our own reading of skin as it is conveyed to paper and canvas, all those famous portraits of people (Biblical or otherwise) surrounded by their own skin, and there is enacted your reader's desire to take up the demure profession of travelling nude, inspiration to Alberta. (We may not know much about art but we know what we like, we Albertans.)

And despite what she reads on the bus – "*Ladies' Home Journal* or *Chatelaine* " (108) – the nude is the reader of the writers of skin; their secret bibliographer. She could, as a sideline (and all those years of teaching literature to students who want to become famous hockey players or incisive brain surgeons have prepared me well), offer a few book club appearances as well, talk about the latest hot American bestseller. Alberta Culture would get a double bang for its buck. A nude lecturer might be even more appealing, the courses will fill quickly, and not only would potential *mahlers* be encouraged but potential literary geniuses as well. Now if only I had some skill as a musician, my credentials would be irresistible.

But the truth is, Henry Kreisel, I long for the profession of travelling nude because I love to travel around Alberta, to "Three

Bear Hills, or Pollux, or Castor" (108) and the temptation of a job that *requires* serious gadding about the province is the real impetus for my willingness to expose my skin to the gaze of the elements and the bus drivers and the keepers of small hotels in towns where the real reason for the hotel is the beer parlour below the upstairs rooms. I know how exhausting the work is, the energy it requires, exuding that aura of drawability, a body available for *mahlerism*, a willingness to turn my limbs to service in painters' frustrated ambition.

In some way, Henry Kreisel, you who made Mahler and who gave him his vision, you also created this nude opportunity for fosterage of an artistic, if not a cultural dream. The business of illusions is an exacting calling, extortionate in nature, laying claim to our best. You gave all you had, elegant grace to this province's articulations, and invented the travelling nude. And through the gaze of lechery and low motives, through the palimpsest of Alberta Culture, there is your vision of the travelling nude, skin and all, strolling with delicious purpose in a February chinook, handbag over one arm, the nude figure site of all initiations, travelling, male or female, bringing with her (and now him too) the graceful touch of culture to the land.

So let me apply to be the travelling nude. Valerie deserves retirement, she's done the job well. I promise to keep carrying the handbag, although I'm likely to stock it with Canadian novels and mickeys of cognac. I will keep the faith, keep travelling to Warburg and Longview and Heisler and Nanton (although because the train has been effaced and bus service is reduced, my route will sometimes be perforce roundabout and I may even have to rent a car). And even if the wind blows cold and my skin feels the dryness of exposure, even if my *mahlers* would rather be painting lakes and mountains, I will insist to Alberta Culture the necessity of my occupation, its invaluable contribution to the growth of perspective and angle, creative fire. Unadorned, without artifice, my hair cut in its usual bob and my legs and armpits unshaven, *au naturelle*, I will suggest composition, *pasticcio*, arrangement, with my very limnable limbs, unvarnished, unarrayed.

And if, Henry Kreisel, I feel a need, once I get to Camrose, to pay a visit to that once-daunting dentist, he who extracted (among others) Valerie's tooth, gave her mouth that unfortunate gap, forgive me. I want only to show him, swinging my handbag, walking easily on my comfortably low-heeled shoes, that the children of Alberta have long memories, that they do not forget the whine of drills and the punitively withheld plastic rings. I will walk into his office, past his leather padded chairs and his lipsticked receptionist gaping in amazement at my jauntiness, right into the office where he has his fingers stuffed into a small person's mouth and say, "See, culture outlives dentistry." And I'll resist hitting him with my purse, that would be assault, all I want to do is make a statement, a bare-ass without a stitch gymnosophical statement that the travelling nude will last longer than he will.

Thank you.

Of Viscera and Vital Questions

The feminist and writing:
An open question following an evocative colon:
A passionate flux:
I always knew my female body had no text, I always knew that words were problematic, inappropriate if not downright dangerous, innately forbidden to me as a woman. The language I grew up within, that I struggle to think and write within, is:
Marian Engel: "indubitably male" (35).
The sex of the bear. And it is, this language, a great shaggy bear, shambling and furry and male, repellent and attractive:
It emanates a "large whiff of shit and musk" (Engel 35).
And I am up to my neck in it, this shitty, sexy language, shaped and developed by a patriarchal frame of reference, excluding me and all women, a male m(y)nefield of difficulties, words capable of inflicting so much pain, and also so much pleasure:
Bound by the limitations of my life/language.
Bound by my first (and other) language (Dutch), an evil/beguiling genie that still ambushes me with its idiosyncratic voice and cultural nuance.
Bound by the language of my desire: fiction, story, the unforgivable and unutterably attractive lie/truth.
Bound by that most mysterious language of all:
Silence.

Which is what every woman shatters when she realizes/knows herself a feminist, when she puts that name to the language of her thinking. From then on, the language of her writing can never be the same:

It has invited itself into a new vocabulary, and without question, a new point of view. She will never write the same.

Adrienne Rich: "The entire history of women's struggle for self-determination has been muffled in silence over and over. One serious cultural obstacle encountered by any feminist writer is that each feminist work has tended to be received as if it emerged from nowhere; as if each of us had lived,thought, and worked without any historical past or contextual present. This is one of the ways in which women's work and thinking has been made to seem sporadic, errant, orphaned of any tradition of its own" (11).

When a woman declares herself a feminist, she becomes part of a tradition, a continuum, and a history, a powerful cacophony of voices and words. She breaks silence:

She refuses to let language man-handle her.

But to arrive at that moment, that identification, that epiphany. The writer, feminist. The feminist writer. An axe that splits the skull. A double labrys:

I remember the moment when I knew myself a feminist writer, when my own skull split open:

I was a student at university, an intelligent and perceptive student, I know. One of my male professors began to deride writing by women – he didn't use the word feminist, and he was rather simplistically focussed on content. "Women," he sneered. "They all write out of their viscera. They never tackle great subjects, like war and peace. That's why their writing will never amount to anything."

The rage that I suddenly felt/knew might just as well have been an axe cleaving my skull. I saw not my life passing in front of my eyes, but the entire history of literature, the narrow, "objective" reportages of men, concerned with their private victories and fears, their megalomanias and neuroses, their lies and their pride. Literature as a game of power and domination, as a gamble for "greatness." The visceral obsessions of men. I should actually thank him for crystallizing my anger and desire.

I was a feminist. I would write. The two came together with a blow.

I suppose that professor has gone on to superannuation, or perhaps he now sneers at feminist literary theory, more out of fear than actual understanding. But his bigoted remark nudged me toward a pertinacious focus on writing:

And feminism:

Although I never deliberately set out to write a politically correct feminist text. Every politically appropriate position is dangerous because one can be appropriated by the position. But my feminism is never far from my pen. I am a feminist:

I am a writer:

I try to live and work as feminist and writer, writer and feminist.

What I expect, yearn for, from my writing/women's writing is an articulation of a secret and uninvented language:

I want to dare to inscribe my body on the page.

I want my characters to speak for themselves rather than to speak some doublespeak version of acceptable feminine thought and behaviour.

I want to trouble the reader – to upset, annoy, confuse; to make the reader react to the unexpected, the unpredictable, the amoral, the political.

I want to explode writing as prescription, as a code for the proper behaviour of good little girls.

I want writing to speak to the reading, articulate woman, make demands on her, refuse to let her sink into a doughy sludge of porridge.

I want to make trouble, I refuse to be held back (Cixous 247).
Women are now happily condemned to a powerful and creative uneasiness.

The exhilerating result of the declared literate presence of feminism is our freedom to question:

To question meaning, history, representation, to question our desires and duties, to question one another. And to re-write, inscribe differently, to re-verse the previously static and perpetually frozen.

That freedom to question encouraged me to write novels about Judith, Ja-el, and Arachne, mythic women whose powerful and active stories have been dismissed or obscured, and worse, mis-read and demeaned. By offering them a textual presence beyond their earlier figuration, I wanted to re-inscribe their tremendously inspiring rebellions, at the same time pointing out that the survival of their fragmented stories gestures toward the imperative presence of women within all mythologies:

Women, damn it, did something. Women made a difference to their time and place, and however much their stories have been fragmented or censored, they demand a reading. And these stories imply that every woman's story (however private and personal and visceral) has importance:

For its anger, for its fierce and unrelenting rebellion, for its unwillingness to eat shit, to be man-handled, pushed around. I love that strength and nerve. Perhaps that is why I want my fictional women to survive, to conquer, to come out victorious, however "unrealistic" their ends may be. *inappropriate*

If we limit ourselves to what is "realistic" in our world (a neat way for the patriarchal system to keep us in line – and then it's unrealistic to be a writer at all), we will always be circumscribed in both literal and imaginary ways. This dis/ease:

To refuse to be contained, restrained, handcuffed.

To invent a women's world.

Of course, no woman's world is clear and one-dimensional. The multifarious experiences of women diverge, expand, suggest, differentiate, refuse to be limited. We are all different from one another, and our variety is richness. Universality is a quick fix, but we are universally different, un/same, with the same concerns and desires:

Only not to be othered from each other, so othered that we get othered out – as in snuffed. All the distinctions we succumb to are man-made, a party line. We cannot permit ourselves to scuttle back to ghettos and divisions, to the perverted sanctity of family, heterosexual orthodoxy, race, class, colour, where we are separated by walls of words, their different meanings differentiating us in too many directions.

Adrienne Rich again: "We have to choose which we will give power to: Diversity or fragmentation" (83).

The privileged (and don't I know how privileged I am now, since I haven't been privileged for very long) need to remind themselves, each other, not to rely on the ascendency of that privilege, but to think themselves into the different position of the different. We (who are white/well-off/educated) need to remind ourselves of the basic principles of affirmative action, of equity building. We have to give difference:

A chance:

The space and place to speak/write her own experience, without encroaching, appropriating, taking over. We need to back off. The world does not belong to me just because I am in it. And I am not black or native, so as feminist or fictioneer I'm not sure I should appropriate difference to aggrandize either my own fiction or my own feminism:

And right now, it might be my job to shut up and listen, or to try to do something concrete to create space for the silenced other, feminist or fictional space to say our story. To know when to back off:

Yet, it also is necessary to recognize that skin-deep privilege is a delusion:

If one is part of a colonized sex, all privilege is a delusion of sorts.

Adrienne Rich again: "For any woman, class shifts with shade of skin colour, but also with age, marriage, or spinsterhood, with a hundred factors all relating to what kind of man she is – or is not – attached to. Class breaks down over color, then is reconstituted within color lines" (293).

And as for appropriating a male point of view, we've been brain-washed with that angle so long, there should be no difficulty. We know theirs more intimately than any point of view we've been able to develop ourselves:

The enormous weight of male story, male measurement, male domination. It's our turn to create some male Madame Bovarys and Anna Kareninas and Molly Blooms. Not appropriation but quite a different matter, a righting of balance, an equalizing of the scales. I believe we are free to create as many bastards and sweethearts and saints and gentlemen and deluded idiots as there are such configurations among men. To revise the overall story, from our point of view:

The visceral story:

Wanting to be told:

Wanting to be heard/read:

Open to criticism:

Our quickness to criticize, our ability to swallow criticism– "take it on the chin":

A mark of our maturity?:

"We're real (wo)men, we can handle it, anything that's dished out."

Another man-handle:

If we criticize each other we don't criticize men:

"Take that, you bitch," even if you are enacting a male-prescribed repression. We are all caught in the same patriarchal frieze:

Frozen in gestures of appeasement, longing, a wish to know difference, even as we are different. Afraid. Trying to get a fingerhold in the labyrinthine hierarchies of oppression, and yet, to quench a deep longing to be accountable, to change myself, my time, the world. The concentric circles of guilt, of justification, of need. All knotted together in an intricate and undecipherable pattern:

All women knotted together irrevocably, however much we may think we are knotted to men, our children, our jobs, threads that cannot be unpicked, that hold us in a tenacious fabric:

Do I consider myself a feminist? Oh yes, yes, yes, yes, despite all the difficulties. Feminism inscribed by the fearful as a dirty word:

"Those damn feminists messing up the world, everything so neatly ordered before."

I think I know what it means, but can I do it? Try, one hour at a time, just try to hear the concert of women, their collective breathing, their manifold hopes. Feminism as desire:

Maybe a feminist because we expect so much of that desire:

Expect feminism to solve everything, when we can only solve one small problem at a time:

Which means that we should be allowed to be mediocre; which means that we should not blame our failings on other women; which means we should not patronize by accusing others of being patronizing. Feminism as a great glittering heaped up pile of possibilities.

Hélène Cixous: "It is impossible to *define* a feminine practice of writing, and this is an impossibility that will remain, for this practice can never be theorized, enclosed, coded – which doesn't mean that it doesn't exist. But it will always surpass the discourse that regulates the phallocentric system; it does and will take place in areas other than those subordinated to philosophico-theoretical domination. It will be conceived of only by subjects who are breakers of automatisms, by peripheral figures that no authority can ever subjugate" (253).

To practise a feminist writing:

Not just to practise myself, my petty observances and fears, but to observe the world of women, and to slide under its skin.

Feminism defined by personal – yes, visceral – experience:

The time I spent:

As a secretary, typing dead letters for dead men and their atrocious grammar but if I corrected it, they corrected it back, and the men were the bosses, baby, who was I to suppose I had the authority to alter the official story?

As a cook, and when the food was on the table the eaters never even tasted it, just turned the salt shaker upside down above it, scraped their plates and left me to do the endless, endless dishes, which is the closure to every fictional feast ever written.

As a baby-sitter, all the obvious elements of diapers and bottles and soothers and naps and toys and crying – but I didn't understand a word of that story, no such thing as a natural instinct for motherhood that I could discover, although that was probably my own fault.

As a hired hand, driving tractors, shovelling shit, milking cows, endless hours of back-breaking work indifferent to who does it, lots of time to tell myself stories, but the main story that it taught me was that I was never going to do another job that I didn't choose to do, which turned out to be another story.

As a theater usherette, telling people to put their feet down, put out that cigarette, stop talking, dragging the drunk and incontinent old men out of their row when the last show was over, shoving them out on the street again, while the stories on the screen categorically denied the stories in the watching seats .

As a reader, reading aloud to a blind scholar, eyes stumbling after long strings of words that all spelled *patriarchy*, a story I could not understand, try as I might, that excluded all my sex into a great absence.

As a girlfriend, staggering along on high heels, combing my hair every six minutes, checking to make sure the eyeliner hadn't run, that there was no lipstick on my teeth. Laughing at everything *he* said, agreeing, letting him make the decisions, permitting my hand to be held, my underwear to be snuck into, all the while thinking, this is a boring story, I can't stand it much more, there's too much fiction here, I'm never going to make it through to the end.

As an immigrant daughter, poor and *different*, a funny name, funny clothes, funny parents, *DP*, the kids called me, even if I was born in Canada, branded with a story I had no choice but to regret.

A feminist practice of writing:

Not to forget all the things that women *do* – keeping the world turning; not to forget my past self as poor and displaced and manipulated. Keep my fictional other sister so that I hear the alterate stories, the incredible diversity of women.

Adrienne Rich: "We must hear each other into speech" (186).

And into writing:

Listenlistenlistenlistenlistenlisten:

Readreadreadreadreadreadread:

Feminism, like writing, is an intriguing unknown, the mystery of what will follow our suggestive punctuations.

Stealing Inside After Dark

Meditate this shared theft
between reader, writer, text. The boundaries of book: patrolled by
writers, inhabited by readers. Fashion all reading from within the
dark house of language and how it is broadcast, disseminated,
bruited about, opussed, you *estafette*.

The book has become its own cell, has booked itself through an
interpreted and imposed (dare you question?) configuration of
writing and reading. Publication, volume, wager: the book rests on
its own spine, its own sewn conclusion of (usually) numbered
pages. It is a prison within a prison, a public space within its
private, a private space within its public, separate and yet of the
world. Potentially, the book belongs to anyone, and yet belongs
only to those who do not own it, but read it, although one
sometimes requires the other. It encloses: pages, words, ideas; it
can, for a period of time, enclose the reader, although only when it
is itself opened. That paradox speaks to the presence of book(s) in
life, to the writing (palimpsestic) of books, their reading
(palimpsestic), and their textual suggestiveness (palimpsestic) as
audience, as substitute and subterfuge, as illusion and artifact. So
be it.

Prescribe a setting, an occasion, a slyly perfect moment when
the writer might examine herself in relation to text. It begins with
confession: the writer *reads* as one who writes, who writes words

with a pen on paper, with fingers on keys. The writer uses various instruments to inscribe these marks you impute recognition to: a fountain pen, a pencil, a typewriter, a computer; even, perhaps, lipstick and incendiary fluorescent paint. A word scratched on skin with a fingernail fades, but it was written; faintly perhaps, but written. Plenty of writing fades, is chewed up by shredders, is erased. The gummily pink block of an eraser is always the most powerful instrument the writer can, even and especially as a child, imagine. Despite stick or strap, rough words or incontrovertible events, when the writer wants to alter her world, past or present or future, she takes to those images a large imaginary eraser, rubs and rubs until the crumbs fall from the effaced white field of the page. This must mean that the writer thinks of all events in words and, with better logic, should be able to dismiss those events she wants to change without bothering to enact the imaginary erasure, the sweep of the arm across page to rub out a pencil's tracery, the necessity of tackling it with energy so that a hole sometimes rubs itself through the paper, the paper too disappearing. But the eraser works, can efface shame, anger, guilt, and even the writer's troublesome and overweening pride.

But back to that required occasion for examination of the writer in relation to the text. Avoid the Gordian Knot of readerly location here, although in some intricate way the reader and the text are two subjects determining each other as objects, or perhaps the continuous act of reading is an assumed objective moment in friction with itself as subjective moment. Thus, put one who writes in relation to the book, the made thing, the after/arte/fact. Do not imagine that the imagined moment is similar for all writers or scholars, but for this particular writer who will serve as your example that moment offers itself visually as a small-paned, square window through which can be seen, by the writer's eyes (probably enhanced by glasses), a room solid with books, a room stepped with bookshelves literally groaning under the weight of books.

Where the writer stands is dark and cold, a chilly autumn evening, while the library that shows through the window is warm, seemingly alight. Or is this already a Victorian novel you the reader reading the writer have entered, and the imagined moment is reading you a transcription of Heathcliff and Catherine lost on the dark moors and staring through a window into the Linton home, full of luxury, but prey to quarrelsomeness, where Edgar and Isabella are " '. . .eating and drinking, and singing and laughing, and burning their eyes out before the fire'" (*Wuthering Heights* 88). Locked out of the library, the writer imagines the wealth within, wishes to be enclosed by its cocoon, wants to steal inside, especially after dark. Wants to be read by the books prisoned in their own cell of library.

The book, or its plural, as cell. The closed book versus the open book. A space to be entered, a secret room penetrated. The book as target, something to be aimed at, moved toward. Bound, printed, sewn, dust-jacketed, end-papered, a made thing, made to be read. Simple? Especially for the writer – the writer who chooses words in order to bring about, eventually, the book: their gathering as signifiers available for printing, binding, sewing, dust-jacketing, reading.

Glutinous statements. "I want to be a writer. There's a book in everybody." As if the two are unquestionably conjoined, and the book's existence a given, a mere play on words, text an unravelling of language that flows from breath or skin. Nothing to it. Playing outside after dark, hide and seek, fox and goose, believing that the door is unlocked, that getting inside the room called text is a mere matter of turning a doorknob and walking in, that getting inside will not require stealth or theft or breakage.

But wanting to write often occasions itself as an unwillingness to read. Welcome to the locked door of the text. While the writer takes the prison of language for granted, is always trying to find a way to enter, so as to permit herself to be read by the text that she wants to write, that she wants *you*, to read.

> *Once upon a time, a time not far away but*
> *present, there are two lovers – do not read them as*
> *male or female, either or both. They have wrecked a*
> *camp cot, a box spring, a futon, several day beds and*
> *a pull-out couch, and they have worn thin a good*
> *Oriental carpet. They are obviously texted by bed,*
> *and their bed-shopping is a determination that the*
> *place of sleep invokes its own reading. They are both*
> *fond of reading, devour books as hastily as clean*
> *sheets, and often read together, one reading to the*
> *other or the other reading the other. Their beds*
> *fail them on account of their own read/ability, and*
> *they are looking for the bed that can withstand such*
> *continued practice. They hunt and shop and check*
> *around and they cannot find a properly readerly bed,*
> *a bed for book-lovers. They are almost ready to give*
> *up, decide that there is no such thing, when one of*
> *them comes upon their bed, in a very trendy*
> *magazine, it must be said, an ad, it must be said, but*
> *very definitely their bed. A wide, inviting bed of a*
> *peculiar make, which rests – it must be said,*
> *regally – on a parquet floor strewn with books: open,*
> *closed, up-ended, piled. The walls are cloistered with*
> *books, old and new, battered and immaculate. The*
> *bed design and manufacture are offered discreetly,*
> *along with a description:*

>> "Design features include slatted springs,
>> adjustable back cushions on all four sides, a
>> pivoting tray for books, breakfast or TV, placed
>> at either the head or foot. A selection of over

250 exciting cover fabrics. Covers are easily
removed for dry cleaning, replacing, or
changing the mood." (Linge Roset
advertisement,   *Elle Decor* 1990)

*The room shown in the picture contains one closed
door, one open door, and what appears to be a
window, as well as a short ladder. There are no books
on the bed itself, although one is laid artfully open on
the "pivoting tray" which swings at either the head
or foot. This is a room for stealing into, a soft cell of
invitation, a reading room. The device of the bed is
almost – but not quite – peripheral to the reading act,
although it offers a reading of the reader-lover (both
of them) with its declension or promise of pleasure:*

"And when you use your bed for something
other than reading, rest assured it's something
you'll enjoy." (Linge-Roset ad)

*Needless to say, the reader and her lover buy the bed,
and read in it, read by the very reading they succumb
to daily: the text of a dark and mysterious place
designed for reading lovers. Booked by books, they
are booking themselves, become the target of their
own reading. But isn't that what we expect of lovers,
if not readers?*

The book declares itself as reading space, a room that permits –
indeed, invites – intrusion. Perhaps it declares other space at the
same time: an armchair, a sleepy cat, a fire. Or whatever space the
book opens as a substitute for time, chronology's spaciousness
profoundly frightening to the temporal reader. The possibilities of

the reading space are endlessly multiple, wonderfully heterogeneous. The reading space refuses and uses the assigned hegemony of ultimate text, the perfect book, the insistent ascendancy of validation.

That ubiquitous game: If you were stranded on a desert island, which book would you want to have with you? The Bible? the Koran? Shakespeare? Goethe? Tolstoy? All male, of course. Collected, of course, an enforced booking of books, assembled and congregated into high authority, the ultimate reading space, bottomlessly nourishing. Here is the book endowed with virtue, promised boundlessness, eternal verité. The text as sacred presence, its own library, no intertextuality necessary or required; the one *perfect* text sanctified and blessed and complete. Stealing inside that exclusive read is a theft, you can stay there forever, in the dark of a hidden passage, a word corner, a shadow line. The power of canonized castaways vested in so very few, and their reading a pre-read determination. It is desert island coronations that are responsible for the status of the book, what it has been cursed to signify: dignity, power, authority, intellectualism, knowlege, all leading toward a productivisation of reading. Which immediately gives rise to the separation of book space from reading, the product incarnate: talking books, hearing books, scratch-and-sniff books, picture books, moving picture books, fuzzy feely books, pop-up books, magic lantern books, shadow books. Not to omit the falsies and cod-pieces advertising their legitimacy, but truly a deception for the reading act: placebo books that open to reveal a cassette tape, a cunning reading light.

Theft of the reverenced form authenticates the slippage of object fulfilled by possession, a "reading" product without the difficult process of actually reading. As if the book permits space for deception: an open book, carved empty and cardboard, containing jam jars or lifesavers.

Although there is multiple space for deception within the

reading space, and while you might question the hegemony of the desert island reading companion, whatever choice the castaway reader would make, it does contain the potentially lethal elements of the read/steal, the derided and valorized constituents that must be linearly displaced in order to become the cell of a book lined with signifying components: the alphabet.

The lovers' alphabet is their exotic bed, with its pivoting tray, its arena for their reading moment, their reading space. You can imagine it easily, since you've been so carefully provided with a pictorial reading of their physical space. They read to each other, they read separately, sometimes one at either end, they read each other, are read by one another. They have stolen inside a read space, uniquely whole, configuration of alphabet. They love reading about other lovers, marking their own expected reading of the other reader. The writer and her lover in Rudy Wiebe's short story, "Seeing is Believing," the until now reasonably effacing writer who has only attempted to place herself in relation to the book, her possible envoy:

"Will you write me a letter every day?"
"Then I'd have time for nothing but to write you letters."
"Really?"
"A good letter, yes."
"That would be lovely. You're a superb writer, but you've never written me an all-day letter."
"I will write you an all-day letter, the most perfect letter possible. Immediately, I will send it to you special delivery, Express as they say, and every day you'll read it all

day and it will tell you everything you want to know of me
and of you and about us, it will be a letter you can read
forever and never grow tired of, absolutely satisfying
whenever you so much as glance at it, you could wear out
the paper reading it so you better put it under glass and never
touch it again until your looking wears it out, wears the
letters right off the paper through glass, I will type it perfectly
on an electric typewriter on hard, white paper and you can
read it forever and it will – "
    "What will it say, tell me, this perfect letter?"
    "Have you put it under glass?"
    "Yes, of course, my eyes are wearing it out. What?"
    "It will say, a b c d f g h i j k l m n o p q r s t u v w x y z.
And I'll sign it, perfectly."
    "Every day I should read that?"
    "Yes, perfectly complete, just arrange it, whatever you
want it to say."
    "I guess that's all carpenters do too, arrange lumber, or
potters mud or painters paint – "
    "Every day I want to say exactly what you want me to
say – isn't that good? The perfect letter."
    "I couldn't even make the word 'love' in your letter."
    "Why couldn't you?"
    'You left out the 'e'." (178-79)

    The alphabet offers a way to begin at the beginning, before the
huge intimidation of library, or even of individual book. Perhaps
the alphabet is a curfew of sorts, an arranged illusion that demands
adherence to time, insists that the stealing inside be recognized for
its collusion of arrangement. The curse of Gutenberg, making the
alphabet fit the page. In Robert Kroetsch's novel, *What the Crow
Said*, Liebhaber, the typesetter anti-protagonist of the novel, must
make the community stories fit the page in the local newspaper,

the *Big Indian Signal*. As typesetter, he is tyrannized by Gutenberg's movable type.

> One morning he left the composing room and went
> as usual up the back stairs to his flat. . . . All the
> capital letters in his collection of wood type were set
> in neat rows, arranged alphabetically. He couldn't
> bear that either. In terror at the domestication of
> those free, beautiful letters – no, it was the absurdity
> of their recited   order that afflicted him:
> ABCDEFGHIJKLMNOPQRSTUVWXYZ – he opened a
> twenty-six of rye and, with immense effort, tried to
> disentangle himself from the tyranny of rote. The U,
> he argued aloud to himself, in the Middle Ages, was
> the final letter, held by the wisest of men to be only a
> rounded version of V. He tried to resay the alphabet
> and failed. I and J, he remembered, were once deemed
> the same: he tried to disregard one in his recitation
> and lost both. He tried again, the simplest changing of
> the alphabet – and heard himself making sounds for
> which he had no signs at all. (69)

The reader and lover, in bed, read Kroetsch, looking
for themselves. They do not feel cursed by Gutenberg,
but blessed. Without him they would be locked out of
this room they have stolen into, its infallible pleasures.
They are only reading, not dying, and that will do for
them, at this moment, that is their safely prisoned
separation from Liebhaber, poor Liebhaber,

> studying his collection of wood type, puzzling with
> his ink-stained fingers the intricate knot of language
> that bound him to death. He hated most the large

capital letters, cut from rock maple, mounted on blocks of wood for the convenience of some printer who had long ago himself been distributed back into the neat chaos. Liebhaber, simply in pain.

He liked to drink while he sat alone at his kitchen table and hated his collection of type. He tried, with the twist of a wrist, to turn an M into a W. Failing at that, he turned a T upside down; but he could read it as easily upside down as upright. He poured another shot of rye into a jar that still wore its bold label: Robertson's Marmalade. He set the word OUT, building from the T he had tried to mock out of meaning. He left the T on the table. He placed the U on a windowsill. He carried the O into his living room. But he knew the word OUT was still OUT. It was the failure to reduce a mere three-letter word to nothing that made him attempt a sequence of illogical sentences; he printed across the linoleum of his living room floor: I'M NOT ALONE. REALLY.

He ran out of punctuation. He found his apostrophes and periods, what few he had, in a shoe box under his bed. He concluded his trilogy of sentences with I'M NOT. Studying his accomplishment, he decided to make a new name out of his initials.

He decided to make the word GLOT and got up from the floor and went into the bathroom for a G and an L. He kept the Gs and the Ls in rows on top of the tank of his toilet, along with scissors for trimming his mustache and his nails. (54-55)

poor Liebhaber, read by "the intricate knot of language that bound him to death." The typesetter/writer, having stolen into the prison of the alphabet, is unable to escape its relentless order, its sharp light. For of course, it is true that Gutenberg obviates the necessity for memory; if one can steal into the book, memory becomes superfluous, it darkens, becomes an outer text. But the lovers and their readers have never minded darkness, so long as there was reading light available. And they cannot believe that they will require memory, having the two most immediate necessities, reading and lovering.

Yes, Liebhaber represents the problematized nature of reading/ writing: the text, in replacing memory, reads the reader, turns an implacable eye upon its reader as though to question her act, and whatever order the text pretends to offer, it distributes the reader back into "the neat chaos." The alphabeticized world has stolen into the precinct of the text, the text that can no longer exist as isolate, inviolate. The very words contained there break apart in the reading; the reader and lover are read by their certain disintegration, for which, of course, the only comfort can be reading. For reading is an act of recognition, confirmation: no wonder it is the purvue of lovers. However much we wish to deny the possibility, book strategy is not passive. The book's mechanism for mastering [sic] its environment is literature's gift for allowing lovers and their readers to re-read/re-love. The page, which Michael Ondaatje's Patrick Lewis from *In The Skin of a Lion* recognizes as the real gift of literature, can be turned backwards. "All these fragments of memory. . . so we can retreat from the grand story and stumble accidentally upon a luxury, one of those underground pools where we can sit still. Those moments, those few pages in a book we go back and forth over" (148). And perhaps there is that final pleasure of the perfect book available to be read over and over again: abcdefghijklmnopqrstuvwxyz. It is everything and nothing. It reads the reader.

And so, like Manet's *Olympia*, the art begins to return the gaze of the audience, the text turns onto its reader an implacable eye. We are unsettled by that gaze, afraid of being read, the reading a power-play to fix, describe, capture, criticize. And the fetish object that we have made of the book turns on the reader, insists on reading back to the imperialistic consumer, not a commodity but an active and reactive implication. The book as product, with its acceptable elements of plot, character, setting, rising action, etc., has revolted, and insists on the process of reading as a never-ending and unclosed continuous act of completion. The book demands reading, the text masters its environment by refusing to be product. As Michael Ann Holly points out, the politics of the gaze are implicit: "looking is power, but so, too, is the ability to make someone look" (395). That ability reads us, and we are afraid of being read, discomfitted by the books that read us. Witness the example of Elly Danica, who in order to write her fictional autobiography, *Don't: A Woman's Word*, read her way into her traumatic historical text of child abuse. She read and read and read, until the texts she read read into her and for her, her own horrifying story. Only then could she deflect the gaze that curated her reading into writing. Truly a way of stealing inside her own text after dark, the darkness of the enforced alphabet of abuse, its curfew on her reading of herself. Curfew: the prevention of conflagration arising from domestic fires left unextinguished overnight. Rape, incest, abuse. Until the text reads back.

On very special occasions, the lovers quarrel over their reading. This occurs when the text reads them, or one of them, or both of them, when the deadly accuracy of the reading is too much to bear, and despite their wonderful bed, their cell padded with books, the lovers are discomfitted. This occurs with Suskind's Perfume; *the smell of the book is acute, it sniffs them out, and they cannot escape its nose, its terrible sensory reading. This occurs with Christa Wolf's* Cassandra, *her prophecies, that she will speak the truth and no one will believe her a reading of her reader who reads her re-writing of the Trojan heroes and their heroic war and must be read within that terrible undoing of the arrogant primacy of Western thought and civilization and literature and religion. Belief: stealing inside the sacred precincts of the razed temple and its bloody replacement. This is only possible after dark, in the safety of the bed in the middle of the book-lined room, although all the books around the lovers, so treasured, so venerated, can be exploded by reading.*

The text's reading of the reader is an uncomfortable moment, that eye turned on the squirming audience – a fetish refusing to be fetishized, reading back to all assumptions. A friend once confessed to the writer, as an interesting story for a writer to know, that he had read *Lady Chatterley's Lover* when he was a young man and had been unable to bear it, had reacted so strongly that he burnt the book, the only book in his life he had ever burnt. His rationale was that it disgusted him but, when questioned, he finally admitted that he was unprepared for his strong sexual response to the book and, as a rather moral and upstanding young fellow, felt he was in some way compromised by his intense reaction. The perfect case of the text reading the reader, without mercy, accurately, a deadly alphabet of recognition.

For the writer too, the text takes over, writes the writer as it reads the reader. This is more than just a determined character refusing to obey the writer's instructions, more than a setting that hops from Lethbridge, Alberta, to Philadelphia, without warning or without reason. The problematic relationship of the writer to her text is evidenced by the increasing presence of the reflexive act of writing *within* the text. No longer does the safe distance of authority, what she controls, exist; the text has become a dark and mysterious place that co-opts her own continuous act of writing. The displacement of that previously hierarchical arrangement – I am the writer, you are the text: you will do what I tell you to do – is no longer so simple. The text has taken over in irefusing to be easily delineated, easily cast into genre definition. Its implication of its readers demands an implication of its writer, and the author, in this strange field, merges and is merged with text, loses her primacy and privacy, her distance from the product of her written words. Perhaps Jorge Luis Borges gestures toward this in his incredible story, "Pierre Menard, Author of the *Quixote.*"

> He did not want to compose another *Quixote* – which is easy – but *the Quixote itself.* Needless to say, he never comtemplated a mechanical transcription of the original; he did not propose to copy it. His admirable intention was to produce a few pages which would coincide – word for word and line for line – with those of Miguel de Cervantes. (39)

Menard's re-writing of the *Quixote* is wonderful: "Cervantes' text and Menard's are verbally identical, but the second is almost infinitely richer" (Borges 42). Why? Because he has been written by his text and its predecessor text, taken over in an elusive re-textualization, casting into complete chaos the traditional relationship that is ascribed to writer and text. This is truly a stealing inside after dark, stealing the extant text, stealing inside it, stealing the dark colonization of text by writer, and the reflexive booking of the text taking over the writer. "Menard. . . . has enriched, by means of a new technique, the halting and rudimentary art of reading: this new technique is that of the deliberate anachronism and the erroneous attribution" (Borges 44). Writing the writer becomes a reading of the reader, stealing inside after dark.

The valorization of creation, together with its literary and historical impact, is thus problematized for both the reader and writer. To write, the writer must permit the text to write her, without attempting to defer to the implacable paradigms of history, literature, and duty. "In women's writing," says Kristeva, "language seems to be seen from a foreign land; is it seen from the point of view of an asymbolic, spastic body?" (166). Stealing into this foreign body, taking it over, infecting it, is one way the woman writer can permit the text to write her, permit her to cross that rigid zone separating text from writer from reader, all frozen by the dictatorship of product. Text becomes process, reading and writing participants in text's process. In order to subvert the division of women's texts and men's texts, the writer will confess that she manages to avoid those product-analytical readers by secret transgressions of the limits of sexual definition. What saves the writer from the interference of censors who want to attribute her texts to her life to her texts is that she does not believe herself a woman, she believes herself a book, a book infinitely re-writable, infinitely re-readable. The book writes her, the book reads her, and that is the author's true textual displacement, the exploded throne of the omniscient and omnipotent creator, the frozen and fixed text, the gullible, passive reader.

The book as thief, always trying to break into a book-lined room, working in the dark, that dark house of language. Wanting to steal eyes.

At the end of Salman Rushdie's *Midnight's Children*, the writer-recorder puts all writing and reading into perspective through a pickling metaphor, valuable for this dissolution of the line between writer, text, and reader.

Every pickle-jar. . . contains, therefore, the most
exalted of possibilities: the feasibility of the
chutnification of history; the grand hope of the
pickling of time! I, however, have pickled
chapters. Tonight, by screwing the lid firmly on to a
jar bearing the legend *Special Formula No. 30:
'Abracadabra'*, I reach the end of my long-winded
autobiography; in words and pickles, I have
immortalized my memories, although distortions are
inevitable in both methods. We must live, I'm afraid,
with the shadows of imperfection. (459)

*And our abandoned reading lovers, reading to one
another on their bookish bookish bed, are they still
engaged in their infinite and unending process? The
writing, the reading text requires the immersion of the
readers into lovers/lovers into readers in order to remain
within that fictional room, that eternally book-lined
room. Whatever forces threaten the text, here is one
act that undercuts its closure: the process of reading.
We are all characters in some huge novel that
someone, somewhere, is reading. Take a book to bed
yourself and perpetuate another text.*

First the Chores and then the Dishes

❧

The family offers itself as a double discourse, especially in any gendered reading. What you can speculate is a halved reading of the family's doubled discourse, its duplicitous side, the side you'd rather not admit, the side you think has vanished with the onset of dishwashers and microwaves and other electrical conveniences, but a reading that still lurks under the auspicies of *family* as something you are supposed to admire, applaud, never doubt.

❧ ❧

In *that* family, work was an open secret; working constant, an on-going presence. It could not be finished, was never over, grew itself into a monster of extortion. Asking for attention. Gave them all the works. They had their work cut out for them just trying to keep up. There was never any question of being *finished*. The tyranny of the present participle: plowing, seeding, spraying, gardening, weeding, haying, baling, loading, stacking, unloading, swathing, combining, trucking, summer-fallowing, rounding up, milking, cleaning, chasing, separating, shovelling manure, shovelling manure, shovelling manure, spreading clean straw, trudgery, drudgery.

Nothing ever done, over, finished. The litany of the western Canadian farm family. All hands on deck, either in field or barn, working.

And then there were always the dishes.

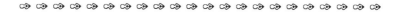

Work is a word that she tries now to skew, to alter. It resists play, rather like a tin cup, merciless and utilitarian. Backwards it is *krow*, and that is its only gambit, its one endearance. It refuses to flirt or even to bungle. It is an *onhandig* (Dutch for clumsy) word, bitter and direct, with the hard *k* of destination. Work. Aloud, it upstages authority, it reifies result. A process toward product, inexorable, unrelenting. Without the 'o' it is still *wrk*, a Siberian stalwart. And yet, she uses it herself, with a kind of perverse pleasure. She is in love with the word's tool, with its potential for deflection.

"I have work to do." (Go away, don't bother me, come back later.)

"I have to go home and do some work tonight." (The evening has an edge of boredom, the company not quite as intense as it might be. The reference to work operates as a subtle rebuke.)

"I have to work tomorrow." (I'm tired and I want to go to bed.)

"I'm working." (Ring my bell, dial my number at your own risk. I am likely to bite your head off for interrupting, that is if I bother to answer at all. I'm working, I'm working, I'm working.)

And then there are always the dishes.

Work is the effort required to produce one's own livelihood, an activity we have canonized through its historical development.

Gerstel and Engel offer an overview: "the Greeks regarded such effort as drudgery fit only for slaves; the Old Testament tradition believed it was punishment for original sin; Protestantism elevated work to a religious duty; and Marx argued that humans created themselves and became distinctively human through freely performed labour" (4-5).

In *that* family, work fell directly into the Protestant category: duty, with a slight edge of leftover Old Testament punishment. And, survival. The opposite end of livelihood, with its tinge of choice. Nothing so elegant or suggestive, so free. Certainly no vocation, or chosen profession. Necessary work, the necessities of work, the work of necessity. Needing to be done, a requirement. Work as a pathway to success, the immigrant drive for achievement. Work baptizing the family Canadian.

They were Calvinists, *that* family, Dutch Reformed Calvinists. Combine that with surviving occupied (for five long years) Holland, and post-war immigration to Canada. How much duty and punishment does any family need? Take it out on work, the final arbiter for all possible choices. Work as escape and justification, work as substitute for language, as its own choreography and destination. Work as an act of immigration itself, an emigrant vice, pleasure in its purity, its particular denomination. It might be called religion.

And then, there are always the dishes.

She tries to remember the first time in her life that she consciously undertook to work, was assigned a job. Assignation. To make illicit. That becomes her talent, the illicitation of duty.

Bringing home the cows from the pasture. Is this work? The leg-stretching hike out to the back quarter, the delicious running sorties after Jessie who wants to stand forever in the slough, the path carved through the bush of poplar and spruce, which becomes without fail the forest of Enceladus, he and all the hundred-armed giants under the green shade, the open stretch behind the bush, its kingdomed roll to the barbed wire fence that marks the edge of property (illicit, this hour for fantasy and dreaming, the open sky, the open prairie grass, the secret darkness of the woods). And yet, the safety of that cow-worn path threaded through the trees as she follows their gently swaying backs home through duty's derelection, and the rising knowledge that the work that offers solitude and privacy is precious. It is a job she offers to do, bringing home the cows. Because it is unclassified, a space for acts of imagination. Illicit acts. That move from fairy tales to conquerings, from delicious fears to sexual delights. Bringing home the cows teaches her to shout and sing, she has the time to test her running, she learns to taste nakedness because yes, one day it becomes necessary to take off her shirt, to let her skin into the air, the orgasm of wind. She is alone out there, she is free to learn how to love herself. This is *not* what bringing home the cows is supposed to teach her: the feel of a fairy's loaf (a round, smooth stone) against her breast, the bark of a tree under a hand that recovers every texture as sexual. She gets the docile holsteins latched into their stalls through a transparent afterwash of pleasure. Is this work? Or is the work peripheral to what really happens when her feet fly over the gopher holes and hummocks, past the tangle of chokecherry bushes and the edge of the marshy slough? In that difference she runs out of herself, out of her skin. Into freedom.

And then there are the dishes.

That family is more practical than hierarchical. There is so much work that it is passed along, divided up, shared around. There is always some left over, it refuses to decease itself. And the nature of *that* family? It has never occurred to them to lament their own erasure, they precede the crumbling of the institution's monolith, its nuclear effacement. They example familial disjunction, emigration as an act of distancing, as a breakage or rift. The successful evasion of cousins and maiden aunts, of dictatorial fathers. For every political and economic reason immigrants offer for their own displacement, there exists an equal number of bastard patriarchs. How do they escape the inexorable hand of the punitive father? Emigrate.

Immigrate. Free to become bastard patriarchs themselves, to establish their own dynasty.

Family as authoritative structure. Shared blood, a shared household (possession there, in the realm of hold), enforced conjunction. The hegemony of the heterosexual couple and their offspring. An economic unit. An accident. A container. A prison. A place within which to conceal crime. Misprision. Misconception, misunderstanding. Universally different; monolithically fragmented. Questions of legitimacy, illegal and surreptitious acts of love.

Breadwinning, housekeeping, natural, biological, functional, common residence, economic co-operation, reproduction. Owned or adopted. *That* family has become its own questioned legitimacy, its own metanarrative. Relational, nurturant. And demanding. Emotional blackmail, the blood's mafia. Enforcement. A prescribed intimacy. Never permitted to escape the silent accusations of toothbrushes, the laboured rectangularity of dinner tables, the battlelines of sibling-shared bedrooms. Conjugular.

Chemical: two or more radicals acting as one. Mathematical:

reciprocally related or interchangeable. Kindred in origin and meaning. Where does *that* family derive from? Then, there are always the dishes.

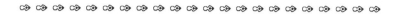

She tries to sort it out, her place within them, the strangely morbid internalization of dutiful daughter/sister. She did not choose them, would never have chosen their particular incestuousness of purpose; and she is certain they did not choose her, convinced *she* was an accident, and accepted only out of necessity, perhaps practicality, another pair of hands to do another set of chores, some of the work that grew and grew. There can be no doubt she is legitimate, genetically inscribed. She knows the tracing paper of feature and gesture, posture and manual extension: her hands link her self to their deliberations.

She thinks of herself as *daughter*. Visible difference. Daw: a jackdaw, a simpleton. A daughter's befittment, when she wants to be as sleek and uncatchable as the otter, its plait of movement through a still-breathing pond, but somewhere in there is an *ought*, a necessity, the auxiliary followed by the infinitive. There is a moral duty in ought, an obligation, propriety, expectation. The silent but waiting mouth of a dot, naught, its circular ambivalence. Open or closed? And the daughter too, open or closed. Perhaps closer to deter, fend off, ward away, discourage. The daughter: dis/couraged. Courage the insistent spirit, intrepid timidity. Properly daughterly, a harbinger of spring. Too much to bear, such ardent investment in a part she plays so badly.

She thinks of herself as *sister*. Her own sister drawing a heavy, invisible line down the middle of the bed. "Don't you dare put one finger over this line." But her sister smells of lemon and honey, and

if she squints at a particular angle, she can read from the page of
her sister's open book, read the forbidden story, that combination
of sinister and stir, their secret siblinghood, although there is no
affection between them, or not much, once she begins to talk, to
talk back, talk about. Both bent to the left, underhanded,
unpropitious. And neither one dextrous.

She thinks of herself as *sister*. Her brothers resist, de/sister her
with their easy contempt, their permissive discrepancies thought
and voiced. "You're just a dumb girl." (Don't worry about having
an inferiority complex: you *are* inferior.) The arm twisted behind
the back, the snowball out of nowhere, the locked insistence of
one's word against the other's. Her brothers teach her otherness,
they pound it into her. They promise her the future: "I'll learn
you – " they say.

Is this work sistering, daughtering? It feels like work, hard work.
The virulence, the tyranny of blood.

And then, there are always dishes.

That family as its own site of development and bereavement.
Family = belonging. And there is not a damn thing she can do
about it, no choice about where she landed up, no choice about
who she got and where, the dice of genes, and the bingo of
conception. To be familied, the concept and the structure verbed,
verbalized, as close as the constituents can find themselves to
being damned, as close as being saved. Kept. Wrapped within.

Leona Gom: "Home is where when you go there they have to
take you in" (227-28) – family that is, no abnegation of the blood,
a dis/own/ment, a repudiation. A name, a bloodtype, a tilt of
cheekbones: physical facts cannot be denied. Family builds dams,

dykes, walls around itself: the nuclear item privatized into its own meltdown and reaction and subsequent explosion. Family wars, fallouts, and pacifications.

While she goes to friends for advice, for affection, for attention, for an isolated moment, separate from guilt and obligation. The family of friends, the ones who take her as she is, without all those troublesome genes, who don't even care about the closet skeletons, the griefs and guilts she bears for too much or too little love. The extended family, its stretched tentacles of aunts and cousins, of the mysterious and inexplicable grandmother who has her name, had it first, who looks so much like her, and who started that family, before the first world war. What affectionate leavetaking of a soldier got that grandmother: a family stretched all over the world, grandchildren as alien and unrequited as that one gasp, one moment of aspiration for intimacy.

And afterwards, there are always the dishes.

She knows her family has given her muscles, an inheritance profoundly useful now, when muscles help her through the rough spots. She can't rely on being ladylike anymore, it won't open doors or get her tire changed, or even give her any answers to the questions that lurk around the back door of history. This is a new binary: muscle and tongue; tongue and muscle. In the old days, there was only muscle, and that was someone else's, a man's. Muscles were off-limits, off-duty for women.

And yet she grows them, easily, bending over a shovel or a pitchfork, wielding a hoe and a rake, serious, required work, not the easy jobs of rounding up cows and collecting eggs, running errands, messages from one part of the farm to the other. Chores.

Clean the cow barn, clean the pig pens, shovel the chop from the truck into the bin. Her arms and legs ache, her back clenches itself under her shoulders. Separate the milk. Lifting the full pails shoulder high, so heavy, so full, having to be careful not to spill the rich thick milk full of cream. And yet, muscles or not, she does, spills enough to catch hell and has to clean it all up, then trudges up the hill to the house and starts on supper because her mother is ironing, peels potatoes and fries sausages, and boils carrots, and sets the table and then the men come in and sit down and say they're hungry, they've been working so hard, and she serves the food and can hardly lift her fork to her mouth at her corner of the family table, and they eat and eat, and shove back their chairs and stretch out their legs while she steps over them to clear the dirty dishes.

Lucky for her, dishes never need much muscle. They hone tongue, and it is there, standing at the piled sink below the window that looks out on the road, that she begins to think of tongue, its wonderful freedom within the mouth, and how it cannot ache the way that muscles do. And she begins to use it, her tongue, her dutiful double, her immigrant prairie tongue.

Her older brother carries the heavy pails of chop from granary to barn, and walking behind him, she hears the wonderfully strange and innovative ribbon of words that accompany his exertion.

"Those are swears," she says to him.

"Right," he says. "I'm swearing."

"Why?"

"Cause it's hard work and I hate doing it."

Muscle and tongue, stretching themselves into new strength, and maybe her muscles aren't as good as his, but her tongue is better, she knows that. Tongue the most flexible muscle.

Replacing the dishes.

CR CR CR CR CR CR CR CR CR CR CR CR CR CR CR CR CR CR CR CR CR CR

Does this go beyond *that* family, to the west, to prairie and sky and the infinite weather? The west as a sprawl of desire, as a gesture of abnegation, a demand for suffering/sufferance? She can't get anywhere out here unless she suffers, and the west comes between the members of a family, filters through their conjunction like the fine dust of a summer storm, the grainy snow of blizzards.

The farm family articulated to the agricultural economy? Petit-bourgeois structure? Household and enterprise under the unrelenting eye of the prairie sky? The inseparability of property from subsistence, of weather from pleasure? Of family from place? She is sure there are no families in eastern Canada, not like the ones she knows, choking and regressive. They are a different sort, polite and well-bred, with plenty of space for circling, for stretching the rope attached to ankles. They call each other darling, a word her family would choke on. "You," her parents say, or "Hey."

Or is *that* family an immigrant delineation? All western families immigrant: if you don't come from the east you come from farther away, a boat load and a train ride across the country away. The western family as transplated organism, a regressive trait. Coming out of the closet. The place to dare family is in the west, a specially arranged unit, suitable to weather and space. The family that prays together stays together; the family that sleeps together snores together; the family that works together –

And then, there are still the dishes.

CR CR CR CR CR CR CR CR CR CR CR CR CR CR CR CR CR CR CR CR CR CR

To develop her tongue muscle she takes to books. If she cannot talk back, if she has to finish her chores before she can hide in the bush, she comes to rely on books. There is a lot of spade work to be done – this is the period when she digs in the garden and the orchard, in the raspberry canes and the windbreak, plants all those ghastly trees and hoes them and waters them and stamps them into the ground. But she develops a method of carrying a pail of water while she holds a book in the other hand, the crook of her arm enabling her to read while she stumbles through her chores. This earns disapproval. Reading is a leisure activity, something she is supposed to do only for fun; although studying is important, reading is heathenish, slightly unsavory, unhealthy.

She wields them both at the same time, alternatively, separately, the spade, the book, the tongue, and the muscle, interchangeable, a slow wearing away of the investment of chores in her life. Her chores are supposed to help the family, contribute to their welfare, teach her discipline, independence, responsibility. They teach her weariness, they teach her repetition, they teach her boredom. The spade stays in her hands without an answer, it falls if she lets it go. She knows that you only need to dig a ditch for an hour to know what it's like for the rest of your life. The book stays in her head, it does not fall, but invites another, more words; it is somehow entangled with the tongue, while the spade relies on muscles, and although she can do both at the same time, muscle and think, she begins to prefer the book as adjunct to chores. For the first time, she wants more dishes; she can read while she washes dishes, but she cannot read while she milks cows or shovels chop. Reading, she makes herself invisible.

And there are always more dishes.

෴ ෴

That family has its own sense of decorum, its own regulations and religion. It runs itself on schedule, on immigrant time, early to bed and early to rise, history has proven that, work first and then relaxation, no stopping until the chores are done, and everybody does his/her share, outside and in, inside and out, tractors and cows and gardens and water, even the dogs must be useful, and if the cats catch no mice they die.

That family eats at particular times, the clarity of schedule, they do not drink or dance and they go to the village for mail once every two days, to the town for groceries once a week. *That* family inhabits the clear destiny of structure, of achievement within environment, the linear narrative at work. An ethic, a myth, a belief beyond religion. Moral philosophy.

That family wades its pilgrim way through the Bible, this is the justification for its relentless schedule, for its indoctrination of the easy-going prairie. From Genesis to Revelation and then all over again. A repeated story, like chores. If she does it often enough, she will never forget how, it will be ingrained on her hands and her back, a tattoo. A rampant and indelible memory, work as evangelism.

Which goes only so far. *That* family lives next door to – what can't even be called a family – those Stangs. Their story winkled out of them over time. Renters, a bad business. Ownership essential to the marrow. Strangely indolent and happy, they are, on summer days swimming in the slough, in winter sledding. You never saw *him*, he was working away. And *she* lay in bed until ten o'clock, that was discovered by the neighbourly intervention of dropping over a dozen eggs. And their suspicious hybridity, which Jeanne (a middle Stang) recited one day in *that* family's kitchen with a glibness and ease that destroyed all notions of family as nation, even preconceptions of Irish-Catholic excess.

"Susy is my little sister, but Jackie isn't my sister, she's my dad's, and Tim is my half-brother, and my dad is my step-dad but my mother is my mother, not Jackie's. And Don is Jackie's sister, and so is Clara; not mine, but Matt and Sally are."

That family squirmed in next-door anguish. The step-family, the second family, the blended family, the melded family, did not yet exist or existed unspoken in the late fifties. And it was worse that they were happy, an outrage such happiness, such cavalier cohabitation.

And their kitchen was the worst, being invited in for coffee, and the kitchen table scattered with dishes, crusted and dry, used teabags lumped on the plates like dead mice.

Mrs. Stang – was she Mrs.? – flipping her hand, "The girls are supposed to do the dishes. But they never do."

There are always more dishes to be done.

She wonders if her version is an embittered one, if she has intervened with her own purpose. Purpose and delight. Which subjected her, narrowed her vision, even while she knew the usefulness of spade and muscle, even while they could not contravene both tongue and book. What is the real story? The subjection of girls? Domestic deprivation, economic exploitation? No. Nothing within a family is exploitive if *everyone* works hard.

Raised as a boy, able to tackle anything, drive a tractor, lift heavy pails. But delineated as girl – inside the house is only women's work, arrangements of domesticity. No matter what you do "outside," inside is always women's work, invisible it seems to the patriarchy's great lie: within the family women do not work. That dangerous source of revolution will the moment when work recognizes itself and refuses to be differentiated, when delight and purpose collide, and escape rides the imagination.

There are always dishes to be done.

ের ের

That family – hers, still hers – believed/believe in work, product, professionalism. Too much spare time and she'd start making up stories, too much imagination affects real work. Creative work is hobby stuff, save it for Sunday afternoons. First the chores, and then the dishes, and then maybe, maybe, she can steal time to read. A ranking of work: physical work, women's work, head work, dream work. Work prevents dangerous thinking, it asks its own questions. And once she's done the chores she can start in on the ironing, the beds, the dishes.

The hierarchies of work still haunt her. She wanted a pen and she drove a tractor. A cloven life: interior/exterior. Refusing to be a woman who enters smaller and smaller rooms until she is crouched on the floor in a corner cupboard. She did the chores, her body still reflects the muscles she made as a child. She came inside and stepped over the long legs of her brothers who had finished their work outside. She did the dishes, gazing out the window at the open road with her hands in soapsuds. She dreamed a story, the story of what women want: to escape the family, to invent themselves past its boundaries and its work. To refuse the seduction of the great patriarchy, its actual and figurative incest. She made herself a construction site, and used spade and muscle and purpose to build tongue and book and delight.

The family is a prism/prison. It refracts all selves into fragments. Promising safety, warmth, comfort, it insists on its own dutiful schedule. It lives women down to the numbed level of the work it creates. It families women into that old position of blood and bone and muscle. Does it dare to acknowledge the blended family and the merged family and the second family and the homosexual family and the family of friends? So far, no. Its misprision is in its refusal to be subject, to lose hold of its pretended objectivity. If it can do that, subject, it might escape the begat clauses of the Old Testament and live again, renewed and positive.

When she was twelve her mother hung a mirror in her room. This may seem a slight occurrence, but in *that* family, where vanity was frowned upon and there was no money for extra furnishings, the mirror finding its way onto her wall was unusual. Was it because she was a girl, a means to reinforce her "nature"? Was it because her mother hoped the mirror would conduct sex education on her behalf and she wouldn't have to offer many explanations? Was it because the mother wanted her to see the muscles she had made doing chores? There, in that silvery reflection, she learned to dance with her double. She forgave herself her gender and the family that she had landed in. She forgave her family. She forgave the west. She even forgave the dishes and those endless hours she spent washing them.

Book and spade, tongue and muscle, delight and purpose, can come together if the body and the body's double escape the family. And in the absence of escape, its disappearing act, the family can re-fashion itself – fluid and proteus will encompass the new genders and the new blood relatives of contemporary dreaming.

There will always be dishes but they need not cloud the mirror of gender. They can dream us past our own devourment: the eating and the eaten western family.

Writing the Immigrant Self:
Disguise and Damnation

☙

This *I* is not a historian or a sociologist but a novelist, a writer of fictions. This *I* is also the first Canadian-born child of post-Second World War Dutch immigrants to Canada, and the novel she has been trying to write for years is an immigrant novel, not so much about her own parents' particular experience but about emigration from the Netherlands and immigration to Canada as profound acts of displacement. The difficulties this *I* has encountered with the *story* of migration and how to translate that story into its own best fiction are encapsulated here. This *I* has learned that the two problems are not similar, are never the same.

Salman Rushdie opens his now-notorious novel, *The Satanic Verses*, with his two main characters on a plane journey between India and the United Kingdom. The plane is taken over by terrorists who blow it up above the Channel, but the two characters, in a symbolic fall, magically survive the plane's explosion and reappear, transformed, on the farther shore, naked as babes, immigrants to England. One character is changed into a devil-figure, grows cloven hooves and a tail, an obvious embodiment of the immigrant as ugly alien. The second becomes an angel-figure, beautiful and desirable, a movie star, clearly the successful and adaptable immigrant. But their representative embodiments are most interesting in that both effect their own transformations and control the ugly or beautiful fictions they become and must subsequently live within. This superlative novel is striking for its treatment of immigration as an act of the imagination willed and performed by the immigrants themselves, even as they are required to function within a defined social and political construct. Rushdie spells out, in the Indian-English binary, what this *I* has repeatedly stumbled against in her attempt to fiction a Dutch-Canadian emigration: the act of emigration enables the new immigrant to fashion her or his own fiction and to live it out. In short, the transformation does not require Rushdie's drastic explosion and miraculous survival but only a journey from one shore to another. The immigrant becomes magician of the self.

Suggesting this idea to actual Dutch-Canadian immigrants evokes the same reaction as blasphemy. Enraged immigrants (now Canadians) have levelled every sociological and historical reason at this *I*, have offered as justification every official pre- and post-immigration argument for their displacement. Of course, the facts and their surrounding commentary are clear and indisputable. Fictions have no desire to alter them. But the nature of statistics is such that they obfuscate as much as they reveal and our reliance on them does not do justice to the powerful secret of the imagined self that immigration offers. Yes, politics and economics and social questions enter into the act; yes, inevitably religion and God do too. But the one faculty that pulls all these elements together in the writing of the immigrant self is the imagination. And the result is such a good *story* that the characters believe it themselves.

But this *I* knows that every story exacts its own revenge. It cites itself as a *worded* event; it also re-stores or stories what might be untold and thus potentially lost. Written, it prefigures a kind of inevitable retribution: the story recoiling on its origins, asking questions of itself, questioning whence it came. And answering to the inevitable questions of those who lived a version of this migratory story: is the story accurate, a "true" story? is the story worthy of its origins? For while the story announces itself, it also insists on evaluating itself, measure for measure, against the passages of actuality. This reflexivity might be construed as the curse of realism; but it can also serve as a proclamation of the ascendency of an ostensible factuality in the immigrant *story*. The plot thickens. And the text talks back.

> *The plot thickens! What does she think she's doing?*
> *Here she's got a fabulous story to write, a natural story*
> *that any writer would give her or his right arm for, and*
> *she's talking about the curse of realism! Fiction, realism*
> *– it happened, period. Why doesn't she just write it*
> *down? She's got enough material to keep her going for*
> *another ten years.*
> *She's looking for the story under the story? My mother*
> *always tells me not to look under stones because I*
> *won't like what I find. Spiders, newts . . . or the wrong*
> *word. A missing word starts it all, that particular*
> *emigration. . . .*
> *He is outside on the road, a brave gesture, he isn't*
> *supposed to be outside the gate, there are soldiers*
> *everywhere, unpredictable, the last few days of the war,*
> *machines roaring and the sky intersectioned with planes,*
> *out on the road beside the round white-painted stones when*
> *a jeep pulls up, squeals to a stop beside him.*
> *"Hey, sonny."*
> *They do not understand each other, no language in*
> *common, a seven-year-old curly-headed kid looking up*
> *at a metallically clinking man, then down at the dusty,*
> *heavy-booted feet that swing to the ground in front of*
> *him.*
> *"Hey, sonny."*
> *They do not understand each other, no language in*
> *common. The man may have a child himself or may*

*have a child that he does not know about. (Where is my
father? But that's a different story.)*

"Hey, sonny, stay off the road, eh. You'll get run over."

*He sounds like a Canadian doesn't he, he is a Canadian;
they have no language in common and the Canadian is not
an immigrant but an occupier, he fishes in the back of the
jeep, a knapsack, pulls out a flat stick and deliberately puts it
into the child's fist.*

"Here. Stay off the road, eh?"

*The jeep bounces the Canadian, over the cobbles, away.
The child goes back inside the gate, takes the stick to his
mother, holds it out for her inspection.*

*"The soldier gave me a stick," he says, as if in
explanation.*

His mother begins to cry.

*He does not know the word "chocolate," has never
heard it spoken.*

"Eat it," she says. "It's good."

*Chocolate is a missing word, an absence. On the strength
of the absence of that word, they will emigrate, remove
themselves from all known language to another language
which has to be learned, slowly, laboriously. But it is a
language that contains the word "chocolate," that will never
lose chocolate's taste. Or so they think.*

*Ah ha, the old chocolate story. It's a classic, you
know. Everybody's got one, a different version but
the same, the big Canadian soldier handing out
chocolate with one hand and freedom with another.*

Fiction, realism – it happened didn't it?

It would be patently ridiculous to write a Dutch-immigrant
novel that worked on the assumption that only one Dutch family
emigrated to Canada between 1946 and 1982, when statistics

plainly insist that there were 184,150 Dutch emigrants to Canada during that time. On the other hand, the best stories preoccupy themselves with individual situations, and the story of an isolated and idiosyncratic Dutch family in a strange country may not be as emblematically or metaphorically inaccurate as statistics would imply. As with any story that must in some way come to terms with historical event, the actual facts provide an overt reference point from which to read the story, but the writer's collusion with fact can become a historiographical collision that offers a far more interesting story in the fictional end.

Thus, every immigrant novel's first concern, transmitted relentlessly to its writer, is, "how do you tell this story?"

This theoretical question has been answered at great length by many writers, from Duras to Marlatt, from Barth to Fowles, from Cervantes to Garcia Marquez, their texts narcissistically observing their own creation and telling and recreating both as part of text's content, but the immigrant story and its entextment or fictionalization demands perhaps a specialized analysis. If that is possible. For the writer writing the immigrant fiction usually writes not from the safe distance of a given exterior (the objective eye/this *I*) but from within the implied fiction – a subjective and hence implicatory position where all the eyes of Argus would not be enough to see the story clearly. And so the problem remains: how to tell this story? What particular angle of the mirror will enable this writer to see a movement that is somehow unseeable in a straightforward reflection?

After years of research, it has become obvious to this *I/eye* that there is not one but there are two stories to work from/with. This *I* is not suggesting here a binary opposition of one or the other, but wants to underscore the doubleness of story, and hence the potential sabotage of text on author. There is first of all the *overt* story. Then there is the much more complex and multi-foliate *covert* story. These stories are the same but differently tainted:

oxymorons of themselves, a contradictory reflectance. They offer every writer a Parisian choice. No matter which goddess he favoured, Paris would have purchased disaster, but his choice has dictated the story we all know, of Helen and Menelaus and a fallen Troy. This choice, again not the either/or of binary opposition, but a choice as to whether this *I* will acknowledge the problematic and problematizing covert story, is the true crisis of every writer who wishes to entext the immigrant experience. Of course, the challenge is to resist the obvious and to find the version that best expresses the magic disappearance and reappearance inherent in the act of immigration, but the pluriaxial nature of the covert story subverts its own conscription. And the process is further complicated by the magic of immigration's terrible complicity with the magic of fiction, seeking to combine its elements in a story of transformation that may be carefully planned and justified, but that nevertheless illusions itself.

Both overt and covert then, the story demands its own revelation and, once written, exacts a peculiar revenge: the tale, like the immigrants it purports to be *about*, versions a disappearing act, results itself a transformation, the staggered illusion of story built on story built on story, one telling resting on the quicksand construction of the previous telling. And here lies the dangerous temptation of immigrant fiction: because immigration itself is a deliberately fictional act, the fiction is a fiction of fiction, a staggered illusion that ultimately capitulates to itself.

The overt story construes the greatest temptation of the two. Its presence and folkloric appeal call to the writer easily seduced by plot. The overt story seems a tempting illusion because it offers itself for transcription, complete with myths and popular refrains, an inevitable rousing of sentimental emotion. This is the vested story, the one quick to blow up under the page, but the story the reader/immigrant desires. It has its own plot summary ready, and this *I* can write action and character to its plan only too easily, with recognizably satisfactory results. If you will forgive a brief and glib reading, this *I* can reconstruct that overt story for this *I* 's experience.

Holland at the end of the Second World War was a deeply stricken and rubbled country. The economy was in ruins, industry was poor, the country was over-populated and congested and opportunities for growth and development very limited. Europe was engaged in a cold war; those who had survived the worst of the occupation dreaded another conflagration. Increasing bureaucracy and government interference made them question their actual freedom: every gesture any citizen made required a permit or at least permission. The Netherlands' trade was nil, it lost its major colony (Indonesia) in 1945, and its prospects as an economic power were not good. Prospective immigrants, most of whom were farmers, minded these things a great deal. They wanted to be their own masters, to own their land, and to live without anxiety or interference. They were, they continue to claim, concerned about the future of their children, for whom they wanted every opportunity. In short, they were ready to be seduced, or at least the story will claim that they were looking for an alternative to what their war-ravaged country and its "creeping socialism" had to offer. The idea of emigration cites these reasons for its own appearance, again and again, as a prototype of the immigrant dream: to find a land of opportunity, unencumbered by a historical moat, where hard work is rewarded by success.

Enter the second half of the idea of immigration, or perhaps it was the first half and the justifications followed the availability of a place to emigrate to. Canada, happy with pre-war Dutch immigrants, needed farm workers. Agriculturalists willing to work as farm labourers would be welcome to apply for admission, provided they were "of good character," "in possession of valid passports," and if they could "pass medical examination and otherwise comply with requirements." Compliance and justification hand in hand, the prospective immigrant (usually a white, Eurocentric protestant) began what would be a particular odyssey and ultimately the enactment of her/his own magical transformation. But the text talks back again.

> *What is she trying to prove? Why can't she just tell the story? That's the way it happened. Compliance and justification! The plot thickens! These damn writers always want to make things complicated. It's an action story, a potential movie, a straightforward accounting of what people did. Enacting their own transformations! Nonsense! They were trying to get from point A to point B. Perfectly simple in any language. Just call it "Travelling to Canada."*

> *Op reis naar Canada*
> *Alles ging in een grote kist. De meubels, de kleren, de boeken, de fietsen, de naaimachine. Bram en Lies waren druk met het inpakken. Over alles in het huis, de schuur, moesten ze prakkezeren, moesten ze praten. Zouden zij het meenemen of niet? Hebben ze wel hagelslag in Canada? En leren jassen? Zullen wij een ander pedaal-orgel kunnen krijgen? Potten en pannen, wollen dekens, en klompen ook. De kist werd vol en eindelijk werd hij dichtgetimmerd.*
> *Zes maanden hadden Bram en Lies Engels les gehad, maar ze waren alles vergeten. Zij wisten alleen potato, en geen woord meer. Zij waren bezig met geld en papieren, met het emigratie bureau, en met injecties tegen Canadese ziektes. Hun twee kinderen, Piet en Rennie, waren te klein om alles mee te maken, maar ze wisten wel dat er iets aan de hand was. Alles was in de war, en niemand wou spelen. Het huis werd leeg. De hond*

*ging weg. De gordijnen werden neer-gehaald. De ramen
werden schoongemaakt. Oma huilde, Opa huilde, en Tante
Mar huilde.*

*Bram en Lies hebben misschien verdriet gehad, maar
ze kunnen zich niet omdraaien. De koffers stonden
klaar. Ze huilden en ze zwaaiden en zo gingen Bram en
Lies en Piet en Rennie naar Canada. Toch waren ze
allebei blij. Canada was het land van dromen,
reusachtig, rijk en onbekend. Ze zouden beren
en bisons zien. En Oma gaf Piet en Rennie een grote zak
snoepjes met haar betraande kus.*

*Het was vijfentwintig maart. Eerst gingen ze op de
trein naar Rotterdam, dan gingen ze met een boot naar
Le Havre. Daar gingen ze aan boord van een heel groot
schip met veel andere mensen. Iedereen huilde. En dan
gingen ze op zee, een ongelooflijk tijd, van Frankrijk
naar Canada. De reis duurde vijf dagen maar schijnbaar
duurde het weken. De zee was stormachtig, en het schip
golfde. Al de passagiers werden erg ziek. Ze konden niet
eten. Ze konden niet uit bed. Lies wilde alleen maar
terug naar Nederland. Maar dar was geen huis meer.
De scheepsdoktor kwam. Als je aan land komt, dan voel
je je veel beter, zei hij.*

*Op een april zagen zij land. Lies kwam uit bed. De
zon scheen. In Halifax gingen Lies en Bram en Piet en
Rennie blij het schip af. Canada was koud, maar het
hemel was blauw en het land vast onder hun voeten.*

*Toen moesten ze op de trein, een zwarte, vuile trein.
Van Halifax naar Alberta is een groot stuk, vooral als
een mens rechtop moet zitten. Vijf dagen en vijf
nachten duurt wel lang op een harde bank. Eerst door de
Maritimes, dan Quebec en Ontario, dan het wijde, lege
land van de prairies. Dag in dag uit stil zitten terwijl*

*Canada voorbij ging. Iedere morgen vroegen Piet en
Rennie, zijn wij er nog niet? Eindelijk, eindelijk, in een
klein dorp, gingen ze uit de trein. Zo'n klein dorp, zeven
huizen, een kerk, een winkel, een pompstation, het
treinstation. Niets meer. Alleen maar een hoge blauwe
lucht met witte wolken. Zand stoof over de straat. Alles
was stil.*

*Zo kwamen Bram en Lies en Piet en Rennie naar
Canada. Zij wisten niet wat morgen zou brengen, maar
zij waren blij dat de reis over was. Zij wachten op de
grote kist, en zij begonnen Engels uit het schoolboeken
van Piet en Rennie te leren.*

*Canada was vreemd, maar zij waren vastberaden om
hier te blijven. Zij werkten en werkten, en langzaam,
langzaam, kwam alles tegelijk tot een goede einde.*

See? Perfectly simple, in any language, even an
obscure Germanic language that belongs to fewer than
fifty million people in the world today.

It is obvious that this story proceeds with its own declensions, a
series of measurable and identifiable iconographic moments that
any historian will recognize from the myriad accounts (oral and
otherwise) available. They can be enumerated as a fixed and
predictable chain. The moment of decision and its hesitations:
shall we go? where shall we go? The preparations: papers, money,
possessions. The family complications: parting's tears and doubts,
the final family photograph, as if departure were an occasion for
death. The journey itself: a crossing calm or rough, and its varying
discomforts. The confusions of arrival in a strange-tongued
country, customs and immigration, sorting out crates and travel
arrangements, and the long train journey to even more distant
destinations. The arrival at the point of settlement: the inevitably
inadequate housing (barns, chicken coops, and granaries) provided

by the sponsoring farmer. The initial adjustment: to strange clothing, food, and language. The eagerly awaited arrival of the *kist* carrying the chosen remnants of the past. Hard work, homesickness, disappointment. But, with a few exceptions, perseverance, determination, and at long last, success, measured by a car, a house, a farm, businesses, children, a rising professionalism, and the establishment of what can perhaps be called a dynasty, in its small way, the emigrant's erasure played out to a satisfying completion of the immigrant's desire for opportunity. A great fiction.

This overt story, and despite summarization repeated elements are recognizable, ascribes to itself a combination of determination, God, and justice as enablement. Any suggestion that the imagination and its concomitant fictionality played an enormous part in the transformational act of immigration, or that the immigrant's self-displacement figures the magic of an arranged illusion, is to invite not only denial but anger. The "truth" of the story's framework is insisted upon, the absoluteness of its characteristics a garniture impossible to shake.

And so, the writer who seeks to articulate that post-war Dutch-Canadian immigrant experience is lashed tightly to the fixed tableaux that comprise this set-piece. The overt story, with its charismatic icons, encompasses all expression, and thus damns both writer and text because its fictional construction refuses any recognition of its own fictionality. This reading is a perverse immigrant reversal of the post-modern presence of metafiction, where the reader is *reminded* repeatedly, in the text, that the reader is not voyeuring realism, but is reading fiction, a process rather than a product, and a process which implicates the reader. As the immigrant practices self-story, the immigrant is practicing but denying self-fiction, and expecting that illusion to hold. Which is exactly the dangerous seduction of the overt story and its endearing givens.

Yet, the invented and carefully polished (all Dutch facades are
kept very clean) composition of the overt story inevitably gestures
toward its opposite, the covert story. And of course, since we all
know about the doubtfulness of fiction writers, this revelatory icon
is the story the fictioneer cannot resist. For it is the covert story that
might suggest itself as potentially "true" in the great fiction of
immigration, the covert story that reveals a great deal about the
magic act of transformation contained within the overt story. Here
we have immigration's *mise en abyme*. But the covert story is
complicated, far more complex than its opposite. Most of all, it is
powerfully taboo.

Any *I* might be tempted to dismiss the covert story as merely
personal, compared to the larger political and social story, but it is
nevertheless the personal, the individual, which occasions the
emigrate/immigrate chameleonic potential. And it is the *person*
who carries this referential crisis out. The personal story thus offers
a projection from/to the official story. And it offers itself in several
ways, which this *I* has tried to pin down, despite the futility of
definition for such a snarled and interwoven signification.

The first *legerdemain* this searching *I* deciphered was the
overlooked obvious, the part of the story that is clear and
unhidden but so obvious that it shelters itself. It suggests itself as
less essential than statistics would argue but, once seen, becomes
an illumination. It revealed itself to this *I* in a personal context.
This *I* has been working on an immigrant novel for some ten years,
during which time this *I* has always known that when her family
emigrated to Canada, her father was thirty-five years old. This *I*
could turn that number any direction imaginable, and yet it
remained covert until a short time ago when this *I* was
complaining to her father about turning thirty-five herself. He
simply stated, very gently, that he was thirty-five when they (he
and this *I*'s mother and their children) uprooted their lives and
emigrated to Canada. A whole piece of what had been until that

moment absent story suddenly fell into place, a piece that has nothing to do with age itself, but with some moment of epiphany that pulls the act of immigration from its safely mythic time to a moment wholly divulgent and articulate, that speaks. Without warning, her father's act entered her time. These discoveries are mostly small fragments, and yes, personal, but their covertness (although the age groupings of immigrants have certainly been statisticized) amplifies their resistance, the text here rebounding suddenly against the imagination, to actualize itself in a temporal ground.

The second *legerdemain* whose existence this *I* deciphered was the secret story, the deliberately hidden and erased story that wishes itself untold, and that uses immigration as a means of camouflage, if not concealment. It frequently jars against the overt story, but the power of the overt story is such that it swamps all of hiding's signage. In all the histories this *I* has read, the many, many immigrant histories this *I* has heard, the secret story is explicitly shunned. It comes out of both public and private realms, but its editing permits the fictioning immigrant to effect the magic sleight of hand enabled by emigration. It is the silenced story: of unwillingness to spend a lifetime looking after a retarded brother or sister, of collaboration with the Nazis during the occupation, of bad debts and love affairs and family feuds. And while the overt story cites official unhappinesses (economic and cultural), it fails to address the *greater* (yes, greater because the personal always takes precedence) unhappinesses. Every repetition of the overt story wishes itself believed as the ideal: that every Dutch immigrant was a heroic member of the resistance, that they all believed in God and attended church, and that they never engaged in crime, doubt, or marital discord. Deviation is considered squalid. Thus, the overt fiction, phalanxed by history's indubitable statistics, is able to enact the magic alteration that the immigrant has illusioned for him or herself. The covert story of the secret self can be left behind with the unwanted furniture, and the overt story, with all its attractive flourishes and historical authority, can be tailored to the individual's private fiction. All of which perpetuates the larger fiction of immigration in a cycle that prefers the fiction to the real but claims that fiction as the real.

The third *legerdemain* that has become evident is not the overlooked obvious or the secret/hidden story, but the absent story. This is the most elusive of all immigration's fiction: it is both the most tempting and the most tyrannical *mise en abyme* because it did not happen. It offers itself as possibility by its absence, and its philosophical demand leans toward the overt story because it is factually provable as never having occurred, but emotionally unprovable by its suggestion. This is the story of the person this *I* would have been if her parents had not emigrated, if this *I* had grown up in South Holland instead of Alberta, and if this *I* had been truly a Netherlander instead of a covert one. This is a story that does not exist, but a story that demands to be told by its lack of existence. This is the story of the writer this *I* would have been if her parents had not emigrated to Canada but to Australia (which is what her father wanted to do but her mother refused point-blank – it was too far, impossible to *imagine*), and so this too is a story that does not exist, but yet demands to be told because it never happened, although it was invented.

Do the absent stories matter? Or does their unknowable covertness prevent them from the possible fictions of transformation? And where do the absent stories fit in the overt history? They persist, they insist on being more than simply the road not taken, they become the emblems of possible farther fictions or what might have been. And then the text talks back again.

She has to be raving. Overt story/covert story. What on earth is she talking about? Failure? There were lots of

*those, immigrants who couldn't hack it, who went
back, now there's a covert story for you, hiding behind
itself. The covert story is the story of snow, of Canadian
understatement, of overwhelming emptiness, of lonely
women. It is not a story of successful agriculturalists
who bought farms and sent their children to University,
but a story that knows displacement for its own sleight
of hand. It has no identifiable group, it takes place
outside the church, and it insists on privacy. And she
should leave it there.*

The fictionalization then, of the immigrant story, is a duet for disguise and damnation. Given the magic propensities of the overt story and its temptations, it is no wonder that the elements of the covert story act as occasions for denial, opportunities to damn potential truths as fictions and to invent a life full of its own fictions. While hubris is hardly a Calvinist difficulty for those elect and elected, the immigrant as magician of the self is not to be denied. To write the immigrant self is to engage in an active fiction, however physical and representative, to fiction a present and a future out of a self-censored past. We all want to escape our autobiographies, and we all insist on reading our best story.

If emigration from the Netherlands and immigration to Canada offer an occasion for superlative story, Biblical in its dimensions, a people of dedication led by God, suffering great hardship to achieve the promised land, practically intergalactic, then let the fiction stand. It is possible to disappear the past and to invent the future. And the grand structure of immigration offers a complete guide, a blessing, and a justification. The immigrant as fiction writer of the self becomes then a creature of the imagination, and practical considerations aside, the inventor of a desired and desirable other.

And woe to the writer who tries to build a fiction on this fiction.

The story extracts its own revenge. And the fiction of immigration becomes a slippery place for the curious struggle between text and life, between this *I* and that.

And then the text does not talk back at all: it is off storying itself into another fiction.

A Re/quisition on Death:

∞

Reading Cassandra

restlessness

Writers must remember to remember that their inevitable position is beneath, below. We stand beneath the stars, the sun, beneath our own pasts and implacable futures. Underground, buried even. Beneath the surface of the skin, be that skin earth or sky, flesh or the imagination, our torrid progenitor. For even abhorring it, the best position is beneath, the proper or appropriate place under, whether that be baseball and the ball or the movement of the trombone's slide and the fingers. These dispositions or arrangements of the body, these positional variants, linguistic and otherwise, whatever brings them about, life or sex or death, or even that most blameable of blames, civilization and what we have written into it – used always as metaphor or excuse, when in fact we are all under the sky of the world and we are all making love to our imaginations, whatever our accidents of birth – become the crucibles of our words.

The writer writes underground, a mole or more appropriately a gopher, tunnelling quietly through the earth of being and language, although the writer might know shamefully little philosophy, just as she is eternally aware of her poverty of expression, that she has not

191

the tongue to celebrate properly the incandescence of this beneathedness. It is *beneath* that points writerly chins toward the stars or the beclouded sky – looking toward heaven, light, the possibility of angels (ah, Handke knows that angels are sad, sad, gloriously sad, that they sorrow with us, that they long for the taste of coffee, however bitter and black it scalds). And the absolute certainty of death.

   All too much has been said and written about death and writing. Too glibly, too easily it slips into our alliances, when we ought to take care, step softly, take care. Michel Butor: "we write to commend and resurrect (pay homage to) the dead" (26); Fraser: "The figures of fiction, both fat and starving, stand in awe of the brooding face of death" (115). Oh yes, we die. Oh yes, we do, we will, we die by inches every day, our skin sloughing itself, our brain quietly losing information, our lungs gasping from the uphill climb, and even that old mother of invention failing us. We fail. But, but, but. We romance dying, rush it into our writing, make a virtue out of death's enunciations and titter through its undoing, thinking, oh what a lovely effect. And fail to die at all, having made that most private of acts a public speculation. But why not? If fiction is one of our minor triumphs over death, why not put death into fiction? And how can writers progress a fiction with death staring into our eyes? The only solution requires that we be not pharasees but scribes.

   And oh, although the flesh dies, flesh never dies, and being flesh must die, and dying must be part of flesh and so part of the fictions of flesh. How then to *restez calme* in that eye of the flesh's hurricane, dying and waiting for death to come? All our feverish embodiments to create on the page an othered life, longer-lasting than our own. This too has been said too much – that writing is an act of need: to make a mark, to say "I was here." The ego paramount and rising. And feeding too the insatiable and prurient curiosity of the reader, the reader's repeated wish to pull away the clothes writers put on words. That reader's search for the writer beneath the stones of words; the writer, never daring to renege on authorship/authordom, wishing to deny the maimed and abortive children who tumble clumsily upon themselves in their need to recount a story. In their surge toward death. For which we all need consolation, reassurance, even assistance, a good push in the right direction. So death has become our high priest, our confessor, our great mystery, our apologist. Everything is dying, we lament, and bend our knee, delighted with doom, its permission for despair.

The writer wishes she could be declared legally dead until a good five years after one of her books is published, in order to escape the consequences of words, both prizes and punishments. That is, of course, a coward's sentiment, but the inevitable follows: the writer is a brave version of coward. The exaggerations of fiction are the purvue of fine cowards, a way to insist our own safe otherness from the extant world. At the same time, fiction offers an almost impervious watchtower from which to snipe at the world, that ungrateful and relentless domain of non-fiction. Which might be why we dwell on death so pleasurably.

But let the writer speak the voice of doom. Death is a theory, the most dangerous of all, and the most tempting. And there is scant label that can accommodate its reach.

So call on death to justify the fiction, to fence the real, to compilate the myriad bad-breathedness of characters who *will* annihilate themselves, come hell or high water, no matter how we insist on them jumping into the one available lifeboat, clinging to the drifting spar (or any kind of wreckage) from the *Titantic*. Death underwrites us all, and gives the nod to realism with a relish the writer should find suspicious. The fact is, death is a fiction, and however we enlist it to our cause, use it to shore up our puny aspirations for immortality, blame our pedantic realism on its presence, death is extremest fiction, the world we do not know, a world we have not entered. Using it as justification for the vagaries of fiction is as great a metafiction as the most common of all possibly common postmodernist ploys citing a mirrored fictionalizing within the mirrored text. And in the fictions of death, we mongers of its potential, we miners, we scavengers on its hopeful bonepile, are as fictional fictioneers as the most insistant of narcissistic poseurs. Yes, death *is* a happy ending (Kroetsch, *Figures in a Ground* 206) goddamn it, the one ending we know but cannot know, the loveliest of endings because it is utterly imaginary and mysterious.

And however much the moral police of fiction may use it as their backstop (dear god, the writer should abjur baseball), its fictional justification is as vindicatory as the theory that would make us see all language double, make us duplicate language into the pinpoint of perspective. We are talking usage here, employment. How close do vindications and propogandas come? And oh, we usurers, we fictional fictioneers, how dare we claim death's territory as our own when it be as theoretical, as arbitrary as the signage of language? Except that we know it happens, and it will happen to us, it will, it will, and perhaps to our words too.

Although the writer should hate baseball, she should hate policemen more. They hate writers too, and all their sort: cheeky young women in fast little snub-nosed foreign cars (however aged and rusty) are fair game, we go too far too fast, never obey the speed limit, the realisms of the road. Refuse to respect authority, and don't think enough on death. There are policemen everywhere, reminding us to watch where we are going, so much so that we may give up going anywhere, take to our feet. The fact is, we have accidents. Not on purpose, of course, but by accident. One vehicle meets another and crunch, crash, there we are, reminded of death again. Which we have narrowly (or not) avoided. But dear god, imagine not trying, not trying to catch the ineffable beneathedness. The police are as inevitable as styrofoam cups, with the same gassy smell, they appear out of nowhere, pull the writer over, write the writer a ticket, give her a warning, sniff her breath, check her pupils: "are you writing fiction or not?"

"No officer, I was just driving down the road, it doesn't matter that I have a pencil (yikes) in my hand, I wasn't writing, I was driving down the road, really, you can trust me, don't you think I know the difference between fiction and reality? Who me? I wasn't writing, I was tracing the world the way it is, driving over it like a xerox machine (whoops, that word is copyright), blotting up its lines and configurations. And the story will end in death, I promise, no more disappearances and redemptions, no more characters who win. They will all die. I give my solemn oath. Yes, I'm sorry I bashed his fender, officer, abuse me please, give me shit, I deserve it, one isn't supposed to have collisions and survive, those are the rules of the road."

And as for the writer's family, they can't be blamed. They talked *reality* to her until they were metaphorically blue in the face, and it didn't do any good. The writer doesn't dare dedicate her books to them, writing is a fictional activity, they go around calling her a professor, which is beneath (back to that again) not her dignity but desirability, and which is more important? The writer would rather die (*sic*) than admit to her own paranoia. And the writer knows death is no joke, several of her dear ones have died, but death's figuration in their story is the greatest potential fiction of all. Oh fiction, where is thy sting? In pretending to be "the real thing" (see Henry James, good old Henry James, for *that*).

But of course, if the writer talks back to the policeman, she's going to get thrown in the old critical jail, charged with a few life-enduring sins, her fictions confiscated, her alibis discounted. *Officer, I was only trying to get to church on time. Sir, my pelvic accomplice is having a baby. I'm very pleased to discern you doing your job, constable; I was testing you to see whether or not you noticed. You can let me go now, I'm in league with your supervisor.*

So much for the real thing, or for those lies, those wonderful lies we compose in order to get ourselves out of tight spots. And death is a tight spot. Death is the lie that we compose to get ourselves out of the tight spot of death. In fiction this becomes a virtue, a moral position. But doesn't such an excuse seem too much like metafiction?

No wonder, then, that the fictional fictioneer starts speculating the critic/policeman in her/his fiction, starts writing the potential commentary on the text composing itself under her/his hand, makes sure the reader notices the structure, plays a few games, underlines a heading here or there. When the critic is policeman we all die, and so do our fictions. Worse, when the writer is policeman, we die before we live and our fictions never breathe, and that, however you slice it, is miscarriage, no matter how much death gets loaded with heaven and universality and that seducer called pain. Robert Kroetsch's "temptation of meaning" (*Labyrinths of Voice* 15) is that we imbue meaning with meaning, our puny gesture toward meaning as close as we can come to getting ourselves, our small measle-minded prurient selves, on the map. *Hah, I've used death here – you can't ignore me now. You'd better pay attention if you know what's good for you, ready or not, I've done it. Even if the character is a cheap shoe salesman who gets hit by a bus when he stops off the curb, I have used the most meaningful experience of all.*

Just so long as we do not use it badly. Writers are cheating, sticky-beaking parrots willing to use anything for the sake of the egocentric fiction. We ought, finally, to dare to subvert ourselves.

In the writer's so-far short but entire life, the text that still succeeds in subverting her pretensions toward death is a novel by the East German writer, Christa Wolf. In this novel, *Cassandra*, Wolf tackles the profession and the responsibilities of the writer with a courage and integrity that few writers dare to dare. It is Homer's story, the *Iliad*, that Wolf re/tells, the penultimate epic of struggle and defeat (or victory, depending on which side you take), but certainly, the ultimate epic of death. We know, of course, that what we have are imprints of Homer, words that created and outlasted and impelled their own recording. For while it is Troy's destruction that brings about its recording (and hence its life), if Troy had not lived, it could not have died, and Schliemann (Wood 246) or no, we would be stuck with the living (*sic*) story. Critics constantly lament that Homer was not more precise so that Troy (its deathbed) could be found, and yet, and yet, realism be damned, it is the lack of verité that gives the dying of Troy its life. Which Wolf addresses by shifting from the death position (Homer's) to the speaking position (Cassandra's).

Every writer knows of the suspicions Cassandra arouses; she is, after all, not the author/bard, but a character in the epic, and a grossly implicated, or shall we say simply unreliable, character, at that. But while archaeology may be able to inform us that the Trojans died, it is Cassandra who assures us that they live, Cassandra whose speaking surpasses the preoccupations of the poet measuring himself (again and again) against death. Even though she dies (of course), and will die again (past the end of Wolf's fiction): is dying always, even as she speaks the version that no one hears, that no one will believe. They are all listening to Homer. And Homer was your basic realist, not to mention that little streak of policeman he exhibited. Which no writer should forgive.

And which Wolf, writing her fiction in East Germany, past the eyes of the censors, refuses to succumb to by taking the spoilage of death into her two fictional hands and showing it for the tool it has become to the orthodox, to the tediously reactionary, to the (male) moral. Writers must grapple with this question of morality, what the language is permitted and not permitted to do. Remember reader, once morality was measured by a skirt eighteen inches from the floor, by the tilt of a beaver hat, by the swift whistle of the birch. To legislate the metafictional act of fiction is to legislate morality, cancel oneself from the whole picture, the act and the responsibility of imagination and the death it can subvert. The great themes of literature (and our imitations of them) are like the famous postcards of the world: they pale beside the scene itself. They pale further beside the physical grandeur that creates what we call, in our quaint nineteenth-century textual way, scenery.

Wolf's Cassandra tells us: "Keeping step with the story, I make my way into death" (3). And Wolf's *Cassandra* enunciates the troubled position of the writer, not a morality, not a coy liaison with death, but a speaking, a shaping of words in the face of death. Writers want the gift of prophecy, whatever its ultimate reward or punishment. Cassandra is a journey and the reader's destination is her voice, the voice of the disbelieved prophetess. Wolf's prose essays (*Conditions of a Narrative: Cassandra*), which explain her voyage in search of the novel, are as much fiction as *Cassandra*. And the doubled narrative that is Cassandra's is as much a story about story as it is a story about Troy.

For the benefit of policemen and moralists, here are the words of Wolf's Cassandra, speaking into her articulated dying:

> The same old story: Not the crime but its heralding
> turns men pale and furious. I know that from my own
> example. Know that we would rather punish the one
> who names the deed than the one who commits it. In
> this respect, as in everything else, we are all alike.
> The difference lies in whether we know it. (14)

ᑤ ᑤ

So the conditions of narrative (that cryptic fiction and its disguises) are established by the reading act as either love or war, regeneration or death.

> *The reader and her reader have taken refuge on a desert*
> *island. Deserts and their islands are attractive to readers,*
> *they emblematize a delectable isolation where reading*
> *opportunities abound. They have escaped to escape, the*
> *reader and her reader, searched out a remote remoteness to*
> *engage in acts of reading intimate as the proximity of letters*
> *on a page. And despite its metaphor, this island is not desert*
> *but oasis, lying beneath the lush equators of green volcanoes.*
> *They are there, the reader and her reader, to argue*
> *themselves a truce, to circumvent the war between speech*
> *and silence.*

Yes, the narrative breaks silence, calls upon itself to speak. The traceries of words, their imprecisions refusing death and outlining the faint suggestion of all possible and potential existence. And reading, the reader assists in this authorship and its devising.

> *The reader and her reader are reading, at last, together*
> *and to each other, a silenced story. Far from the brokeraged*
> *inheritance of Europe, on an island reefed with jasmine*
> *and coral, they lie beside the Indonesian sea and read, with*
> *the ocean hissing quietly beyond the range of the page.*
> *They are finally free to imagine the legendary seer who*
> *read the unwritten text of future, to read her unseen and*
> *invisibled world, its long war and longer recuperation,*
> *to read past the permutations of Homer and Aeschylus.*
> *The reader and her reader are reading Christa Wolf's*
> *Cassandra. It is, unfortunately or not, a translation of Christa*
> *Wolf's German* Kassandra *and* Voraussetzungen einer

Erzèhlung: Kassandra, the text which emerged from Wolf's
series of five "Lectures on Poetics" which she delivered
(yes, read) at the University of Frankfurt in 1982. Neither the
reader nor her reader can read German, so they are nervous
of the extent to which they are relying on the translative
reading of Jan van Heurck. But there is nothing to be done
about their mutual inability to apprehend German, and they
remind themselves that reading a translation merely
reinforces the translative act they are engaged in, the
palimpsestic layers between their reading and Cassandra
herself – the implied text of her being and disappearance.

It is a long war, Cassandra's, ten years until all enemies depart
from the site of her last seeing. And Christa Wolf, keeping step
with her story, makes her way into Cassandra's articulate death
(*Cassandra* 3), locates the last moments of Cassandra's life, there
outside the Lion Gate at Mycenae, before she meets her death by
sister, Clytemnestra's reading and Cassandra silenced in her
prophecy. No systems of poetics here (141), only the final
resonnance of her fading voice speaking into the world's
subsequent silencing. Her cry before she dies, before her story
dies.

The reader and her reader keep step with Cassandra's
story through Wolf's conditional narrative. It gains a dreadful
hold over them, their reading: the procession of thralldom,
patriarchal imposition, into the 21st century where they rest,
albeit far from home, albeit in a quixotism of white monkeys
and banyon trees and merus, rice grains and the Barong.
Despite the warm nights and the gamelan *orchestra, the*
reader and her reader find themselves standing outside
eternal palaces locked in prophecy, reading ahead to their
own impending deaths, their own narrative erasure.

Cassandra silenced in her prophecy.

And yet, Cassandra. Historical Cassandra, Priam's daughter, Hecuba's daughter, Helenus's twin, Apollo's acolyte, Eurypylos' wife, the mother of twins, speaker of the unspeakable. The speaking subject "rendered powerless and voiceless" (Pickle 34). And Wolf's Cassandra figuring the writer, the woman writer invisibled: never believed, sounding into a void, the disbelieving silence of the gap. "The first recorded female voice" (Pickle 34), Cassandra speaking out of the immediacy of her own annihilation. Pilloried by her desire for difference, it is ironically her enemies the Greeks who anoint her as prophetess, who spread her fame with their own oral profligacy. "It was the enemy who spread the tale that I spoke 'the truth' and that you all would not listen to me" (*Cassandra* 106).

Wolf narratives Cassandra's vocation as resulting from the volatile cross-contamination of the personal and the political, crucibled in the deception of war, a pre-planned (male) war embarked upon to test new weapons, to test old strengths. Wolf speaks Cassandra through that old, old war – between silence and speaking, deception and articulation – speaking through her. The Trojan war. All war. Wolf signals the cusp of victory as residing in the power struggle between said and silenced, an exhortation to sight. Her speaking Cassandra proves silence, makes afraid, and then becomes the object of fear, reversal of speaking subject.

> *The reader and her reader cannot bear Cassandra's terrible silence. They follow in the steps of her grief, trembling as hey read; even as they are baked by the Balinese sun, they turn pale at Cassandra's heralding. They want to read her a different story, triumphant, not the requisite enactment of madness and death that comes out of the obverse of the narrative the reader and her reader know only too well: the famous narrative of Cassandra's*

*brothers and enemies, their male triumphs and heroic deaths.
The reader and her reader know the burning sea, the thin
thread of life (21), the blindness of sight (27). They lie beside
a sea iridescent past the island's coral necklace; in the
darkness of the humid nights, their fingers practise Braille;
they lift their eyes from Wolf's page to Gunung Agung, the
navel of the world. They want to read Cassandra back to
life, offer her the rehab-ilitation of belief, hear her voice.
They read her free from her captors and her victors, even as
they know the long, long-fingered death of victory's helpless
text (8).*

For Wolf's Cassandra is not silent but speaking to this reading.
She relates the whole sorry mess in retrospect while she waits –
ruefully sorry that fate has not put them on the same side (42) – for
Agamemnon's wife to finish butchering him and to get around to
her (77). Imprisoned in a woven willow basket, a spoil of war,
Cassandra unravels that war's origin, its dreadful maintenance.
Caught in the moment before her sacrifice, Cassandra effects
forgiveness in her narrative memory, acknowledges her part in the
death of the house of Troy, and recognizes the unthinkable, that
the world is not over but will continue beyond Troy's destruction
(11). And yet, the terror of her memory re-reading this epic is
precisely the unsilencing that bespeaks a prophecy.

*Defense becomes a position that the reader and her
reader are forced to occupy. They cling to the small cuticle
of knowledge that stays the world as they have always read
it. They have not bargained for this reading, of themselves,
of each other, of Cassandra. She seems too much a metaphor
for all speaking and listening, all reading acts. And here,
in this presumably idyllic geography, tinctured with
cinnamon and copra, elephant grass and cypress, it is almost*

*impossible for the reader and her reader to remember what
they are supposed to know and believe about western
civilization, the ancient cornerstone of what they have
learned as culture. A great historical war continually
re-enacts itself, but here it is called the* Mahabharata, *not the*
Iliad. *And yet, and yet, poets embellish, and heroes spill
blood to avenge their inevitable honour, while Cassandras
bespeak the inevitable outcome of such overweening pride.*

And Wolf's Cassandra has an acerbic tongue, naming the
discrepancies that practise Troy, that puppet the Trojan men. Priam,
"less than the ideal king, but. . .the husband of the ideal queen"
(13) becomes "increasingly unapproachable and obstinate, yet
controllable all the same" (20-1). This is what war does to men,
moves them from childish stubbornness to fear and finally
brutality. Cassandra reads them: Paris (bag or pouch), "a stranger to
himself" (45), Hector-Dim-Cloud (110), Achilles the brute (74),
Troilus the sacrificial victim (74), the wily Odysseus, and Helen a
word, non-existent, a lie invented to justify the temptation of war.
The ascension of male over female in megaron and council, in
language and appetite. Cybele outlawed, and slowly, slowly, the
desires of men prevail.

> But what kind of place were we living in then? . . .
> Did anyone in Troy talk about war? No. He would
> have been punished. We prepared for war in all
> innocence and with an easy conscience. The first sign
> of war: We were letting the enemy govern our
> behavior. (64)

In the name of honour and because of feared loss of face, the
Trojan war begins, continues and continues, reading itself into an
inexorable history, an altered gender balance. War and its death-

text robs women of the sacred right to freedom and choice, makes
of the Trojan women prisoners and chattels.

> Priam the king had three devices against a disobedient
> daughter. He could declare her insane. He could lock
> her up. He could force her into an unwanted marriage.
> This device... was unprecedented. Never in Troy had
> the daughter of a free man been forced into marriage.
> This was the last extremity.... When it happened it was
> clear to us all: Troy was lost. Now I, Hecuba the queen,
> the unhappy Polyxena, all my sisters, indeed all the
> women in Troy, were seized by ambivalence: they had to
> hate Troy even while they wished it the victory. (78-9)

Wolf's declension of Cassandra's reading, her prophecy,
ascribes to patriarchal desire the deadly poetry of heroic death.
And no logic, no Amazon, not even potential love, seems able to
stop the dreadful reading of hero as inevitable killer.

> *The reader and her reader have been reading* Cassandra
> *aloud to one another. They listen and read; their eyes open
> to both words and tears. Wolf's taut voice speaks across the
> thick-grained sand, even to the gently breaking waves barely
> twenty feet from their finally browner feet, Canadian feet
> that have scant experience walking in warm, thick sand.
> They escape Cassandra and her cry of woe by following the
> gamelan, its clamourous tongue floating over distance, past
> the trunks of bamboo and palm trees in an effortless call.
> The male and female drums (kendang) heart the music of
> the* cengceng – *hand cymbals – while past every sound
> resonates the steady beat of the* kempli. *The higher notes are
> frequent, piercing, and it is a relief to the reader and her
> reader to hear a descent to the lower range, breaking against*

*the insistent wave of the kettle and gong cacophony. If they
did not have pliable imaginations, the readers would
consider this music jangling, harshly melodious cacography.
The hands of the musicians work instinctively, without
notation, the eyes of the player fixed on space, intricate
embellishments of air. The reader and her reader search
for a potential text to read there, find none, only alluring
discordance. They are forced to return to* Cassandra.

And so, Wolf's Cassandra is caught in her own story: "nothing I
could have done or not done, willed or thought, could have led
me to a different goal" (3). Death, finally, as goal, a choosing?
Despite the insistence, "the durable stuff of those cords that bind
us to life" (4). It is Cassandra's story that articulates, answers the
question of why writers court death, strive to achieve the gift of
prophecy in their reach toward their readers. Cassandra's desire:
"To speak with my voice" (4).

*Cassandra's voice reaches the reader and her reader in
the Balinese darkness, past the ages and ages of unrelenting
time that have held woman's voice in thrall. Cassandra, in
the past tense, speaking the past tense, articulates collective
memory, the too much forgotten and too much seen. And
under the sway of the* gamelan, *the reader and her reader
stumble over Cassandra's trance, the rhythm of
abandonment, convulsion and exorcism. Watching a*
Sanghyang Jaran, *the famous wooden horse reappears, and
then the reader and her reader read the monstrous idol for its
trickery, the burning that pours from its belly. The dancer
rides the hobbyhorse around a bonfire made from coconut
husks, and his feet, caught in his trance, dance through the
fire. Afterwards, when the tiny dancers are shedding their
gold brocades, and the* gamelan's *bronze and bamboo*

*resonance is stilled, the reader and her reader reach their
fingers out to touch the brown and unburned soles of the
Sanghyang Jaran dancer. These dances exorcise evil,
infections of the spirit, through trance. The reader and her
reader touch each other's feet all night, amazed at their
unboundedness, their freedom to read the far reaches of the
manifold world.*

The horse is brought inside Troy's walls. Blood flows. Fire burns.
Cassandra raped. Troy falls, wailing terribly, its death cry. "Who
will find a voice again, and when?" (8). Wolf poses her question
and then goes on to answer it, with Cassandra's voice, and her
articulated desire:

> "Clytemnestra, lock me up forever in your darkest
> dungeon. Give me barely enough to live on. But I
> implore you: Send me a scribe, or better yet a young
> slave woman with a keen memory and a powerful
> voice. Ordain that she may repeat to her daughter
> what she hears from me. That the daughter in turn
> may pass it on to her daughter, and so on. So that
> alongside the river of heroic songs this tiny rivulet,
> too, may reach those faraway, perhaps happier people
> who will live in times to come." (81)

Words recorded into the great suffering of silence, and Wolf's
Cassandra finally speaking the silence. Destruction immortalizes
the prophesier, the predicted doom ensures the reputation of the
doomsayer. All words, words, Cassandra surviving only in words,
and Wolf's story of her living, her careful day-to-day deductions,
written onto the open page of her terrible absence. The inflexible
truth, Cassandra having spoken into silence, that now, now, is
finally broken.

*The reader and her reader have reached the question they
are searching for an answer to, reading Cassandra silently,
aloud and to each other. Cassandra reads them, and in their
double reading reverberates a deep vibration that reaches
them, overreaches her ages and ages. The speech act of
reading, silent speech, words recorded into the great silence
suffered, everything in Cassandra, in the reader and her
reader, finally dumb. There in a land that pretends to be
paradise, they hold each other, read each other's bodies
through the back and forth of printed lines, the grained
signature of a lost and longed for touch.*

If "War gives its people their shape" (13), Cassandra's war still
rages, full of captive women and their keening. Wolf's efforts to
disentangle them from the deathliness of death and the incipient
wrappings of destruction speaks a survival, a way to emerge from
the long seige, from the journey to captivity, from the waiting
vengeance. The words Cassandra speak are for all readers: "Today
I will be killed" (14). The narrative closes, the story dies.
Continuous killing, this incipient death that presses itself close, that
follows writing determinedly as a shadow.

In an extended war, one comes to fear one's own aggression as
much as the enemy's: such pent-up silence a long encompassment
of what all know but dare not speak. The undesired truth: "they
accused [Cassandra] of needing to see people turn pale" (19).
While she, through Wolf, dances away from that speaking, the
paleness brought on by knowledge. The condemnation of the
blunt statement, a forthright coming forth. One small utterance in
the many silences. Cassandra calls to Cybele for help, asserts her
presence, the goddess of Caverns. The cavern of the mouth as the
source of celebratory outcry, and yet a cave closed, enclosed,
waiting to speak. The incipient cry of primitive and savage earth.
And what does it mean, the inarticulate cry articulated finally, in its

need to be released? Waiting there, Cybele, in the cave of the mouth, a shriek, a delicious song: witness.

And Cassandra, never more alive than in the hour of her death, speaks as a writer. "We were grateful that we were the ones granted the highest privilege there is: to slip a narrow strip of future into the grim present, which occupies all of time" (134). She continues as a witness (22) to all sacrificial victims, written or not, read and unread. In the cave of the mouth rests a long preparation for war.

> *The reader and her reader are past any reading, aloud or silent. They lie on their beach chairs and hold their faces toward the warming sun. They can hardly hear themselves breathing, hardly dare, having read aloud their terrible difference, to interpret that prophecy. They make a pilgrimage to the Besakih, mother temple of all Bali, hoping for an exorcism. This is no corrupt and falling Troy, no war here built on a facade of invisible stolen women. Under the clinging frangipani leer demonic stone faces, and inside the temple proper the chairs for the visiting deities assure the reader and her reader that the temple here is not neglected or violated by sword or pretext, it is merely waiting for its odalan, for the opening cockfight, for the multi-coloured pyramids of fruit and rice, the chanting and the Pendet dance. At dawn the festival will sway to a close and the satisfied deities will depart again.*

Cassandra's desire, to change sex, the male privilege of external genitals, dangerous testosterone, accompanies the imparting of her questions. But must one "become like the enemy in order to defeat him" (30)? It is not birth that makes the character but the stories that the character is told, the story of fear followed, tracked through its animal scent, unlike the counting economists who list numbers, statistics of betrayal. Women threatened by their own narrative, enactments of poverty and speechlessness. It does not do to cry over spilt stories, unfathomable political realities. Wait for the moment to speak. Hold still within a ring of silence. Enact what is necessary, and then live with those enactments; these are the paradigms of rebellion. Cassandra's voice sticks in the throats of reading women, throttles itself in the darkness of unspoken truth, the terrible knowing that comes only with speech, that yet will speak.

Ah Cassandra, killed by Clytemnestra, sister hand against sister hand, when the real contentiousness arises from the other: men. Who prevent sister and sister from reading the same story. But Cassandra remembers that "Forgotten people know about each other" (47). Here rests the peculiarity of tribal, gendered, and sexual memory, its invisible and delicate knowledge.

> *The reader and her reader finish* Cassandra, *and hesitate*
> *in their appraisals of its narrative. They have both, each,*
> *secretly, wept, listening to the other reading Cassandra's*
> *eulalic deathsong. Balinese stories are inscribed on leaves*
> *of the lontar palm cut in strips and preserved between pieces*
> *of wood. So perishable too does Wolf's story seem without*
> *victorious victors, the heroic heroes abandoned on the stage*
> *of their dying, in an unread paroxysm of brutality and lust.*
> *The reader and her reader join hands, walk slowly beside*
> *the curl of water touching land. Their ears are full of*
> *invisible, of vanishing words. Their mouths are full of silence.*
> *Their eyes lift to the sacred volcano, the navel of the world,*
> *shrouded in mist, keeping its mysterious self to itself. They*
> *pass themselves on the beach, and stop to listen, finally past*
> *death, to their own story reading them.*

Works Cited

Atwood, Margaret. *Survival: A Thematic Guide to Canadian Literature.* Toronto: Anansi, 1972.

Blanchot, Maurice. *Le Livre à venir.* Paris: Gallimard, 1959. As quoted in Todorov, Tzvetan. *Genres in Discourse.* Translated by Catherine Porter. Cambridge: Cambridge University Press, 1990.

Borges, Jorge Luis. "Pierre Menard, Author of the Quixote." In *Labyrinths: Selected Stories and Other Writings.* New York: New Directions, 1964: 36-44.

Brontë, Emily. *Wuthering Heights.* Harmondsworth, Middlesex, England: Penguin Books, 1965.

Buch, Hans-Christof. *The Wedding at Port-au-Prince.* London: Faber and Faber, 1987.

Michel Butor as quoted by Leon Rooke. "is you is or is you ain't my baby: canadian fiction against the headwinds." In *Brick: a journal of reviews,* 33 (Spring 1988): 24-30.

Carroll, David. *The Subject in Question: The Languages of Theory and the Strategies of Fiction.* Chicago and London: University of Chicago Press, 1982.

Cixous, Hélène. "The Laugh of the Medusa." Reprinted in *New French Feminisms: An Anthology.* Edited by Elaine Marks and Isabelle de Courtivron. New York: Schocken Books, 1981: 245-64.

Conrad, Joseph. *The Secret Sharer.* London: Signet, 1910.

Cooley, Dennis. *Soul Searching.* Red Deer: Red Deer College Press, 1987.

Croce, Benedetto. *Aesthetic.* Translated by Douglas Ainslie. London, 1922.

Danica, Elly. *Don't: A Woman's Word.* Charlottetown: gynergy books, 1988.

Dubrow, Heather. *Genre*. London: Methuen, 1982.

Engel, Marian. *Bear*. Toronto: McClelland and Stewart, NCL, 1985.

Findley, Timothy. "The Tea Party, or How I was Nailed by Marian Engel, General Booth and Minn Williams Burge." *Room of One's Own*, 9, 2 (June 1984): 35-40.

Fraser, Keath. "Notes Toward a Supreme Fiction." *Canadian Literature* 100 (1984): 109-17.

Frye, Northrop, et. al. *The Harper Handbook to Literature*. New York: Harper and Row, 1985.

Gerstel, Naomi and Gross, Harriet Engel. "Introduction and Overview." In *Families and Work*. Philadelphia: Temple University Press, 1987.

Gom, Leona. *Zero Avenue*. Vancouver: Douglas and McIntyre, 1989.

Grass, Günther. *The Tin Drum*. Translated by Ralph Manheim. New York: Random House, 1964.

Hernadi, Paul. *Beyond Genre: New Directions in Literary Classification*. Ithaca and London: Cornell University Press, 1972.

Hirsch, E.D. Jr. *Validity in Interpretation*. New Haven and London: Yale University Press, 1967.

Holly, Michael Ann, "Past Looking." In *Critical Inquiry*, 16, 2, (Winter 1990): 371-96.

Hutcheon, Linda. *Narcissistic Narrative: the metafictional paradox*. London: Methuen, 1984.

____. "Incredulity Toward Metanarrative: Negotiating Postmodernism and Feminisms." In *Tessera*, 7 (Fall 1989): 39-44.

James, Henry. *The Real Thing and Other Tales*. New York: Books for Library Press, 1893 (republished 1991).

Jiles, Paulette. *Sitting in the Club Car Drinking Rum and Karma-Kola: A Manual of Etiquette for Ladies Crossing*

Canada by Train. Winlaw, B.C.: Polestar Press, 1986.

Joyce, James. *A Portrait of the Artist as a Young Man.* New York: Viking, 1971.

Kohler, Pierre. "Contribution à une philosophie des genres." *Helicon*, II (1940): 137-39.

Kreisel, Henry. "The Travelling Nude." In *The Almost Meeting.* Edmonton: NeWest Press, 1981: 107-20.

_____. *Another Country.* Edmonton: NeWest Press, 1985.

Kristeva, Julia. "Oscillation between power and denial." In *New French Feminisms: An Anthology.* Edited by Elaine Marks and Isabelle de Courtivron. New York: Schocken Books, 1981: 165-67.

Kroetsch, Robert. *Gone Indian.* Toronto: New Press, 1973.

_____. *What the Crow Said.* Toronto: General Publishing, 1978.

_____. *Alibi.* Toronto: Stoddard, 1983.

_____. and Diane Bessai. "Death is a Happy Ending: a dialogue in 13 parts." In *Figures in a Ground.* Saskatoon: Western Producer Prairie Books, 1978: 206-15.

Laurence, Margaret. *The Diviners.* Toronto: McClelland and Stewart, 1974.

_____."Introduction" to Sinclair Ross. *The Lamp at Noon and Other Stories.* Toronto: McClelland and Stewart, NCL, 1968: 7-12.

Lukacs, Georg. *The Theory of the Novel.* Translated by Anna Bostock. London: Merlin Press, 1971.

Mandel, Eli. "Houdini" in *Crusoe: poems selected and new.* Toronto: Anansi, 1973: 70.

McClung, Nellie. "The Black Creek Stopping-House." In *The Black Creek Stopping-House and Other Stories.* Toronto: William Briggs, 1912: 9-109.

Miller, J. Hillis. "Narrative." In *Critical Terms for Literary Study.* Edited by Frank Lentricchia and Thomas McLaughlin. Chicago: The University of Chicago Press,

1990: 66-79 .

Munro, Alice. *Lives of Girls and Women.* Scarborough: Signet, 1974.

Neuman, Shirley, and Wilson Robert. *Labyrinths of Voice: Conversations with Robert Kroetsch.* Edmonton: NeWest Press, 1982.

Ondaatje, Michael. *In the Skin of a Lion.* Toronto: McClelland and Stewart, 1987.

Pickle, Linda Schelbitzki. "Scratching Away the Male Tradition: Christa Wolf's *Kassandra.*" *Contemporary Literature,* 27,1 (Spring 1986): 32-47.

Rich, Adrienne. *On Lies, Secrets, and Silence: Selected Prose, 1966-1978.* New York: W.W. Norton & Company, 1979.

Roethke, Theodore. "I Knew a Woman" in *The Collected Poems of Theodore Roethke.* New York: Anchor Books, 1975.

Ross, Sinclair. "The Painted Door" in *The Lamp at Noon and Other Stories.* Toronto: McClelland and Stewart, 1968: 99-118.

Rushdie, Salman. *Midnight's Children.* London: Picador Books, 1982.

____. *The Satanic Verses.* London: Viking, 1989.

Ruttkowski, Wolfgang. *Bibliographie der Gattungspoetik für den Studenten der Literaturwissenschaft.* Munich: Max Heuber Verlag, 1973.

Shields, Carol. *Various Miracles.* Toronto: Stoddart, 1985.

Sydney, Sir Philip, *Apologia Poetica. (An Apologie for Poetrie.)* London: Clarendon Press, 1907.

Todorov, Tzvetan. *Genres in Discourse.* Translated by Catherine Porter. Cambridge: University of Cambridge Press, 1990.

Toye, William, ed. *The Oxford Companion to Canadian Literature.* Toronto: Oxford University Press, 1983.

van Herk, Aritha. *A Frozen Tongue.* Mundlestrup, Denmark: Dangaroo Press, 1991.

____. "Biocritical Introduction." To *The Robert Kroetsch Papers, First Accession: An Inventory of the Archive at the University of Calgary Libraries.* Calgary: The University of Calgary Press, 1986: ix-xxxviii.

____. *Places Far From Ellesmere.* Red Deer, Alberta: Red Deer College Press, 1990.

Wallace, Bronwen. *People You'd Trust Your Life To.* Toronto: McClelland and Stewart, 1990.

Watson, Sheila. *The Double Hook.* Toronto: McClelland and Stewart, 1959.

Wiebe, Rudy. "Seeing is Believing." In *The Story-Makers.* Toronto: Gage, 1987: 174-92.

____. *Playing Dead.* Edmonton: NeWest Press, 1989.

Wolf, Christa. *Cassandra: A Novel and Four Essays.* Translated from the German by Jan van Heurk. New York: Farrar, Straus and Giroux, Inc., 1984.

Wood, Michael. *In Search of the Trojan War.* London: British Broadcasting System, 1985.

Author/Critic Index

Aeschylus, 199
Aristotle, 36, 102
Atwood, Margaret, 25, 35, 38

Blanchot, Maurice, 38
Borges, Jorge Luis, 152-53
Brontë, Emily, 141
Buch, Hans-Christof, 16-17,
    33-34
Butor, Michel, 192

Carroll, David, 39
Cixous, Hélène, 132, 135
Conrad, Joseph, 18
Cooley, Dennis, 85-98
Croce, Benedetto, 21

Danica, Elly, 150
Dubrow, Heather, 21

Engel, Harriet, 159
Engel, Marian, 86, 129

Faulkner, William, 35
Findley, Timothy, 86
Fraser, Keath, 192
Frye, Northrop, 36-40

Gerstel, Naomi and Gross,
    159
Gom, Leona, 163
Grove, F.P., 86

Hernandi, Paul, 13, 21
Hirsch, E.D., Jr., 30
Holly, Michael Ann, 150
Homer, 196-97, 199
Hucheon, Linda, 39, 107

James, Henry, 195
Jiles, Paulette, 69-70, 74-77,
    79-82
Joyce, James, 13-14

Kohler, Pierre, 13
Kreisel, Henry, 119, 121-26
Kristeva, Julia, 52, 153
Kroetsch, Robert, 20, 30,
    57-67, 86, 146-48, 194,
    196

Laurence, Margaret, 89
Lévi-Strauss, Claude, 39
Lukas, Georg, 13

McClung, Nellie, 85-98
Mandel, Eli, 36-37, 119
Marx, Karl, 159
Miller, J. Hillis, 102
Mitchell, W.O., 86
Munro, Alice, 111

Neuman, Shirley, 20

Ondaatje, Michael, 38, 57,
    66-67, 149

Pickle, Linda Schelbitzki, 201

Rich, Adrienne, 130, 133-34,
    137
Ross, Sinclair, 85-97
Rushdie, Salman, 153-54, 173
Ruttkowski, Wolfgang, 18-21,
    24

Shields, Carol, 45-46, 53-54
Sydney, Sir Philip, 30

Todorov, Tzvetan, 14, 36

Wallace, Bronwen, 101-17
Watson, Sheila, 57, 62-64
Wiebe, Rudy, 6, 9, 86, 145-46
Wilson, Robert, 20
Wolf, Christa, 196-209
Wood, Michael, 197

Aritha van Herk

Aritha van Herk was born in central Alberta and studied creative writing at the University of Alberta, where she received her Master of Arts. She first rose to international literary prominence with the publication of *Judith*, which won the Seal First Novel Award and was subsequently published in the United States, the United Kingdom and Europe. Following the publication of *The Tent Peg*, she was selected as one of Canada's most promising young writers in the 45 Below competition. Her third book, *No Fixed Address: An Amorous Journey* was nominated for the Governor General's Award for fiction. In 1990, her fourth book, *Places Far From Ellesmere* was released and she also edited the acclaimed anthology of Alberta writers, *Alberta Re/Bound*. Aritha van Herk's short stories, articles, essays and reviews have appeared in publications such as the anthology, *Alberta Bound, The Globe and Mail, Calgary Herald, Chatelaine, Elle, Canadian Fiction Magazine* and *Canadian Forum* among others.

She lives in Calgary where she teaches Canadian Literature and Creative Writing at the University of Calgary.